Earliest Childhood Memories

Earliest Childhood Memories

VOLUME 1:

Theory and Application to Clinical Practice

ARNOLD R. BRUHN

Foreword by Robert W. Holmstrom

New York
Westport, Connecticut
London

Library of Congress Cataloging-in-Publication Data

Bruhn, Arnold R.
    Earliest childhood memories : theory and application to clinical
practice / Arnold R. Bruhn ; foreword by Robert W. Holmstrom.
       p.   cm.
    Includes bibliographical references (p.
    Contents: v. 1. Theory and application to clinical practice
    ISBN 0–275–92699–0 (v. 1)
    1. Early memories. 2. Cognitive psychology.   I. Title.
BF378.E17B78   1990
153.1'2—dc20   90-7079

British Library Cataloguing in Publication Data is available.

Library of Congress Catalog Card Number: 90–7079
ISBN: 0–275–92699–0

First published in 1990

Praeger Publishers, One Madison Avenue, New York, NY 10010
An imprint of Greenwood Publishing Group, Inc.

Printed in the United States of America

The paper used in this book complies with the
Permanent Paper Standard issued by the National
Information Standards Organization (Z39.48-1984).

10 9 8 7 6 5 4 3 2 1

Copyright Acknowledgments

The author and publisher gratefully acknowledge permission to use the following copyrighted materials:

Bruhn, A.R. (1984). The use of early memories as a projective technique. In P. McReynolds and C.J. Chelume (Eds.) *Advances in Psychological Assessment* (Vol. 6.). San Francisco: Jossey-Bass, Inc. Reprinted with permission.

Bruhn, A.R. (1985). Using early memories as a projective technique. The Cognitive-Perceptual method. *Journal of Personality Assessment, 49*, 587–597. Reprinted with permission.

Bruhn, A.R., and Bellow, S. (1984). Warrior, General, and President: Dwight David Eisenhower and his earliest memories. *Journal of Personality Assessment, 48*, 371–377. Reprinted with permission.

Bruhn, A.R., and Bellow, S. (1987). The Cognitive-Perceptual approach to the interpretation of early memories: The earliest memories of Golda Meir. In C.D. Spielberger and J.N. Butcher (Eds.) *Advances in Personality Assessment*, (Vol. 6). Hillsdale, New Jersey: Lawrence Erlbaum Associates, Inc. Reprinted with permission.

Bruhn, A.R., and Last, J. (1982). Early Memories: Four theoretical perspectives. *Journal of Personality Assessment, 46*, 119–127. Reprinted with permission.

DENNIS THE MENACE® used by permission of Hank Ketcham and © by North America Syndicate.

Eisenhower, D.D. (1967). *At Ease: Stories I Tell to Friends*. New York: Doubleday. Reprinted with permission.

Last, J., and Bruhn, A.R. (1983). The psychodiagnostic value of children's early memories. *Journal of Personality Assessment, 47*, 597–603. Reprinted with permission.

Last, J. and Bruhn, A.R. (1985). Distinguishing child diagnostic types with early memories. *Journal of Personality Assessment, 49*, 187–192. Reprinted with permission.

Mayman, M. (1984). Early memories and character structure. In F. Shectman and W.H. Smith (Eds.), *Diagnostic Understanding and Treatment Planning: The Elusive Connection*. New York: John Wiley and Sons. Reprinted with permission.

Mayman, M. (1984). Psychoanalytic study of the self-organization with psychological tests. In F. Shectman and W.H. Smith (Eds), *Diagnostic Understanding and Treatment Planning: The Elusive Connection*. New York: John Wiley and Sons. Reprinted with permission.

Meir, G. (1975). My Life. New York: G.P. Putnam's Sons. Reprinted with permission.

Meir, G. (1975). My Life. London: Weidenfeld and Nicholson. Reprinted with permission.

To my mother, Paula M. Bruhn—
Thanks for the memories!

The important things are what we remember
after we have forgotten everything else.

Virginia Axline

CONTENTS

FIGURE AND TABLES

FOREWORD

That psychological assessment has experienced a genuine and widespread resurgence of interest and development over the past decade or so has become a commonplace observation. After years of criticism and suspicion, psychological assessment has reemerged as an area of active growth and productivity. The resurgence can in part be traced back to the first appearance of the Halstead-Reitan Neuropsychological Battery where remarkable success was demonstrated in the evaluation of brain dysfunction. The publication of DSM-III with objective and explicit diagnostic criteria encouraged the development of highly-reliable structured interviews and emphasized the need for and utility of well-developed (reliable and valid) psychological tests. In the area of personality inventories, we now have available the first major revision of the MMPI. In projective testing, where basic concerns with reliability and validity have plagued user-researchers for years, Holtzman's development of a rigorous inkblot procedure and Exner's Comprehensive Rorschach System stand as successful and important efforts in the improvement of these complex instruments, along with current efforts to improve narrative-apperceptive techniques.

One important procedure that has until now remained somewhat outside this general renaissance in psychological assessment is the Early Memories technique. The idea that recalled early memories might be useful in understanding personality and psychopathology first received systematic (though varied) treatment from Freud and Adler. Although interest in early memories among practitioners and researchers has waxed and waned, early memory techniques have persisted as less-developed and informally-used assessment devices, with interpretive principles often rather arbitrarily tied to a particular or favored theoretical viewpoint.

Rahn Bruhn has changed all of this with the publication of his extensive and thoughtful treatment of early memories and the formulation of the *Early Memories Procedure*. I was fortunate enough to watch some of his ideas develop through his supervision of graduate student research and by sitting in on his classroom presentations. I rapidly became convinced of the extraordinary clinical value of his procedures and equally impressed with the range and thoroughness of his efforts. He has, in addition, provided for the *Early Memories Procedure* a theoretical framework (Cognitive-Perceptual theory) that seems broad and flexible enough to be both useful and acceptable for almost any interested clinician and/or researcher: what might be called a "user-friendly theoretical framework." The result is a very powerful assessment procedure that, most importantly, speaks directly to the clinician's need for informed and effective intervention.

The cause of early memories has been greatly enhanced by the publication of this volume: the basic ideas are clearly and cogently presented, the theoretical framework carefully scaffolded, the case materials convincing and truly illustrative, and the rationale for the *Early Memories Procedure* fully developed. For anyone interested in early memories—whether beginning graduate student, experienced practitioner, or clinician researcher—this is the place to start!

Robert W. Holmstrom

PREFACE

I began my research with early memories (EMs) in 1972 at Duke University. To my amazement, I found that there were no books on EMs. "How could that be?" I remember thinking. "Most personality theories are constructed with early childhood experiences as the foundation. How can it be that no one has written a book on the subject?"

Not only were there no books on EMs, there was little useful information on how to assess or interpret them. Some of Alfred Adler's papers were helpful conceptually in clarifying the function of EMs, but Adler's interpretations often seemed inscrutable. I found myself perplexed about such phrases as the individual's "fictive final goal was . . ." or that the client was lacking in "social interest." The only way I could accept Adler's interpretations was to embrace his theory of personality, which I found useful to a point, but narrow. Nor was Freud very helpful. Freud's attitude toward screen memories is summarized by one of his closest colleagues, Wilhelm Stekel (1950), who observed in his autobiography: "Psychoanalysis has taught us to distrust our memories. Freud proved that there are screen memories, pictures of an apparently harmless nature behind which vitally important experiences lie hidden. How can one separate the chaff from the wheat, how distinguish false memories from accurate ones (p. 27)?" Thus, what was really important was hidden and, short of extensive analysis, would never be discovered. Freud's position effectively buried early memories as a legitimate field of scientific inquiry for the better part of a century.

As I became more familiar with the literature and began to apply these ideas in my clinical work, I came to accept Munroe's (1955) contention that EMs should be considered the first projective test. Gradually, I revised my initial view of EMs as veridical records of events past (which is often true) and began instead to conceptualize EMs as a *projective test of autobiographical memory*. It was nearly impossible to convince my colleagues of the correctness of this premise since, at a very human level, *we tend to regard EMs as actual historical events* not subject to the customary rules of projective interpretation. My associates would often argue with irritation, "But Bruhn, that really happened. I *know* it did. I've discussed it many times with my mother." It was difficult to convince my colleagues that *these positions were not mutually exclusive*—event *x* may have really happened *and* the construction of event *x* can be interpreted as projective data. I began to appreciate how difficult it is for us to escape the concrete reality of our lives and to wonder instead why we even recall event *x*— as opposed to *y* or *z*—which hypothetically could be remembered just as easily. Although Adlerians have argued the projective nature of EMs for over seventy years, this concept has never entered the mainstream of psychology.

In addition to several publications from Adler and his followers, I discovered in those graduate school years a handful of papers that stimulated my thinking. A brilliant dissertation by Malamud (1956) provided some clues as to how one might do effective research with EMs. Mayman (1968/1984a) crafted a beautifully written paper for his presidential address to the Society for Personality Assessment and several papers related to using EMs for psychiatric diagnosis and the assessment of object relations. Wolfman and Friedman (1964) contributed a fascinating paper on the EMs of impotent males that also spoke indirectly to the issue of how an EM scoring system might be constructed. Langs and Reiser (1961) also described a thought-provoking, psychoanalytically oriented scoring system.

Despite these pleasing oases, the EM field in 1972 was largely an intellectual desert. Although Adler had established EMs as a major cornerstone of his psychiatric evaluation procedure, his method of interpretation never caught on broadly with individuals who did not accept his theory of personality. Unfortunately, no other school of psychology routinely used EMs as part of its initial evaluation process or psychological assessment battery. In addition, research on EMs was in disarray. The last literature review had been completed in 1948 by Waldfogel as an introduction to a research monograph. Short of an exhaustive and time consuming literature search, there was no way of knowing who had done what in the field. With no scholarly book available to organize the area, researchers were on their own. The review of the research literature in Volume II is the first comprehensive review since 1948.

I realized that if I wanted to understand EMs, a vast amount of work would be necessary. I began with the problem of constructing an EM scoring system that would shadow the Rorschach systems. I decided to take an empirical approach since I had no idea of how an EM should be scored. Somewhat arbitrarily I decided to construct a system to predict the Rotter Internal-External Locus of Control stance (which was devised to assess the extent to which an individual was willing to take personal responsibility for his actions) from EM data. I reasoned that if I could successfully predict an individual's control stance, I would also learn much about constructing an EM scoring system. In hindsight, the control stance variable was a fortuitous place to begin since accepting responsibility for the outcome of significant events in one's life is a necessary element in successful psychotherapy. Using EM data to predict Rotter stance also permitted the concept of personal responsibility to be viewed through a very different lens. The findings from this study suggested that a broad spectrum of beliefs was correlated with attitudes regarding personal responsibility, and that many of these had no obvious relationship to personal responsibility. As anticipated, the study (Bruhn & Schiffman, 1982b) helped to generate some ideas about how an EM scoring system should be constructed (Bruhn & Schiffman, 1982a).

Meanwhile, the theoretical literature was so scattered that it was difficult to know how people had made use of EMs. It was therefore necessary to undertake some organizational work. Toward that end, one of my graduate students and I put together a review of theoretical literature (Bruhn & Last, 1982), dividing these papers into one of four theoretical groups. The fourth group—Cognitive-Perceptual theory—represented my first attempt to follow up on research that I had done at Duke and to formulate an independent theory of EMs that was grounded primarily on memory theory (see also Bruhn, 1984). A considerably expanded version of Cognitive-Perceptual theory appears as Chapter 3 and a review of the three other models (Freudian, Alderian, and ego-psychological) comprises Chapter 2.

One of the unique features of Cognitive-Perceptual theory is that it is designed to address how personal growth and personality change impact memory organization. By contrast, classical psychoanalysis focuses primarily on drives and drive reduction, Adlerian theory assesses the individual's fictive final goal, and behavioral theory looks at various techniques, such as reinforcement schedules, that can be used to induce people to modify their behavior. Cognitive-Perceptual theory begins with the undeniable fact that many people can and usually do change (why else do psychotherapy?) and focuses on how such changes come about from a cognitive viewpoint. When we are interested in change, EMs become a natural yardstick as they remind us how we see things *now*. When significant growth occurs, such changes are reflected in the choice of EMs, something that I had observed with my clients. When a client worked through an issue, his attitudes changed, his perception of himself and others changed, and the world appeared different to him. These changes were also reflected in his selection of EMs. Either his EMs changed entirely, or his previous EMs were altered to reflect his current world view, just as Adler and his colleagues (e.g., Mosak, 1958) stated would occur. This was heady stuff indeed for a young clinician to witness! After the excitement of this "discovery" wore off and I began to consider what I had observed more carefully, I concluded that I should not be surprised if memory theory was valid. Why should we hold on to old beliefs and old perceptions when such data only clutters up long-term memory and makes it difficult to use new insights and understandings? With nothing but antiquated EMs remaining, we would be forced to remind ourselves, "Yes, I used to perceive things to be thus and so, but now I see things differently." Such an organization of autobiographical memory would be tedious and cumbersome and not especially *adaptive*. In retrospect, it was surprising to see such recollections recede from awareness only to the extent that I retained an archaic perception of EMs as an accurate historical record. If nations revise and rewrite their histories to reflect present beliefs, it should come as no shock that we as individuals do the same with our own histories.

Once Cognitive-Perceptual theory was formulated, it was necessary to illustrate how the theory could be used to make clinical assessments. Along with Sheri Bellow, then a graduate student with an interest in EMs, I began to do work with the first EM of Dwight David Eisenhower to demonstrate what could be learned about this American president. This paper was published in 1984 in the *Journal of Personality Assessment*. The response to the paper was so encouraging that we began to work with the memories of another national leader—Golda Meir. Meir's memories (Bruhn & Bellow, 1987) enabled us to explore matters that had never before been discussed in the EM literature, such as the role of family myths in relation to EMs and the purpose of an afterthought in an EM. Eisenhower's and Meir's EMs are discussed in Chapter 4.

Before the Meir paper was published in 1987, the *Journal of Personality Assessment* invited me in 1985 to describe my work with EMs in more detail. This provided an opportunity to expand and elaborate certain parts of Cognitive-Perceptual theory, including the role of affect and axioms in memories. The article also included the first process interpretation of a set of EMs. This material is incorporated into Chapter 4.

Meanwhile, my empirical work with EMs continued as I attempted to devise a scoring system for EM material. Another of my graduate students, Sharon Davidow, became interested in the EMs of delinquents, so we decided to formulate a coding system that would permit us to distinguish delinquents from nondelinquents. This collaboration produced some promising results (1983) that led to a much more sophisticated, computer scored, system, (Davidow & Bruhn, in press). The predictions were extremely accurate, which suggested that EMs were well suited to performing this particular task. A follow-up pilot project comparing criminals with a history of adjudicated aggressiveness to those with no such history also yielded near perfect predictions, increasing my hope that we were on the verge of something important. Unfortunately, progress has been slow because we lack easy access to an adequate sample.

Although the creation of a general purpose EM scoring system is in process, Jeffrey Last, another of my graduate students, and I began to work on this problem from another perspective in the early 1980s. Last devised the Comprehensive Early Memories Scoring System (CEMSS) and tested it on groups of latency aged children who differed in degrees of maladjustment as well as type of pathology. The CEMSS passed its initial test easily, outperforming three clinicians who were experts in the clinical use of EMs (Last & Bruhn, 1983, 1985). My own subsequent clinical and empirical work has led me to revise the CEMSS. The CEMSS-R(evised) appears in Volume II.

One obstacle that has impeded progress in the EM field has been the lack of a standard stimulus and methodology, something analogous to the cards and directions for the Rorschach and TAT (Thematic Apperception Test). I therefore began to experiment with various written procedures, beginning with the spontaneous EMs (the earliest memory, the one that comes to mind next, and so on) only. With time, I began to see the necessity of including directed memories (e.g., memories of punishment, school, a traumatic experience, or an inappropriate sexual experience) when my long-term clients began to introduce issues not appearing in their previous spontaneous EMs. The Early Memories Procedure (EMP)—consisting of five spontaneous EMs, a particularly clear or important memory (lifetime), fifteen directed memories of various types, and several rating scales and open-ended questions—was field tested in 1987 and published in 1989. This procedure covers all major clinically relevant areas of autobiographical memory and offers a wealth of information otherwise unavailable in a standard psychological battery. It is particularly helpful in identifying major issues that the client is actively trying to resolve now, issues that the client is often too afraid to convey to his therapist face to face. To my knowledge, the EMP is the first and only projective test of autobiographical memory available to the practitioner. This procedure is discussed in Chapter 5.

Meanwhile, I continued to explore the best use of EMs in treatment. This matter was first raised in my graduate training via a story related by my dissertation advisor, Harold Schiffman. Schiffman discussed a client with whom he had worked for some time with but a modicum of success. The man had a poor self-concept and little self-confidence. Like Joe Bfilstix in *Li'l Abner*, he walked around under a perpetual black cloud and appeared to attract misfortune. He was small in stature, frail in physique, and homely in appearance. His first memory recreated a long-ago incident in which his mother was shaking her finger at him and berating him for something. He recalled her face contorted in anger and his feelings of profound hopelessness, worthlessness, and shame. He could not even recall what had prompted the rebuke, but the scene was a familiar one—the voiceless, angry face of his mother berating him.

Schiffman conceptualized the first memory as a template through which present experience is filtered. Whenever present experience is discrepant with key elements of the template, the experience is not retained. In other words, we tend to recall only those events that are consistent with our world view. Psychologically crucial schema are recorded on the template. Schiffman believed that his client's prognosis was poor unless a key schema on the template could be altered.

Schiffman decided to hypnotize his client and attempt to alter what he suspected was the key pathognomic element. He elected to preserve the EM as it stood except to tell the client that, although his mother was berating him in the memory, she loved him nonetheless. The problem, as he explained it to the client, was that her communication skills were grossly deficient. She wanted the best for him but lacked the skills to help him. When the client awoke from the hypnotic trance, he had the confidence of a fire-breathing dragon! No longer did he doubt his self-worth. His mother *had* loved him all the time! When asked if he wanted his old memory back, the client said, "No," with absolute finality. He then strode confidently out of the room, never to be heard from again.

Although other interpretations are possible, I believe that Schiffman was able to transform a critical schema. In one bold stroke, he permitted the client to feel loved and valued without having to devalue his mother. He could now believe that she truly loved him but had simply failed as a communicator.

As my clinical experience with EMs grew, I conceptualized what Schiffman had done as reframing a key axiom (see Chapter 4), or pivotal belief in his self perception. Basically, the axiom could be paraphrased as, "I am worthless, inadequate, and unlovable." For individuals who operate with such axioms, anything worthwhile that is accomplished is discounted unless the therapist can help them find a way to reprocess their experiences in a less self-defeating manner. In most cases, it is not the experience itself that defeats us, it is how we construct the experience. For instance, if I fail an important math test as a youngster, I can process that experience as "I am a terrible math student" or as "I need to spend more time on my math." Once the first construction takes hold, even successful experiences are misprocessed—"I scored 100 percent on my math test, but that was because the test was easy, not because I am a good math student."

I also came to realize that we use EMs to keep track of issues in process. Each of us is a creation in the making. What we ultimately become at the end of our lives is directly related to how quickly we master a finite list of life issues involving mastery of self (impulses, fears, etc.), interpersonal relationships, and various skills crucial to an increasingly urbanized society (assertiveness, communication skills, etc.). Early memories present an opportunity for us to monitor our own progress since they tend to focus on battles won only after a great struggle (see Eisenhower's earliest memory in Chapter 4 for example) or major issues that are unresolved and currently in progress (see Chapter 3). Once I understood the function of EMs, I could then decipher the meaning of Schiffman's berated boy memory.

The client was trying to convey that he could not progress with his life until he could find a way to feel adequate and loved. Schiffman helped him do that. When he did, the problem was resolved, and treatment was no longer needed, at least not for that problem.

As Schiffman's case illustrates, hypnosis can be used effectively with EMs through either direct or indirect induction methods (Milton Erickson's writings are filled with examples of the latter). The key, often, is to identify intentions in EM process—the client's and that of others in his EMs. In the previous example, it was important to clarify the intention and the feelings obfuscated by his mother's actions. But there are many methods besides hypnosis that can be used with EMs in treatment. These include: (1) separating cause from effect in EMs to clarify how the world operates; (2) reframing an EM so that the preconscious need is expressed; (3) and helping the individual understand from his EMs what is unfinished in his life and how he can resolve these issues. This topic will be discussed in Volume II as part of treatment applications.

In many respects, the field of EMs and autobiographical memory can be likened to a map of America during the sixteenth century. It was known that America existed, that it was important, and that many exciting discoveries lay ahead. In the 1990s, we know just enough to realize that EMs are important although we are not sure exactly how. Much more remains to be discovered before this map is complete. Although this book promises nothing more than the beginning of the adventure, I hope that you will find it a journey worth taking.

ACKNOWLEDGMENTS

So many people have contributed to the birthing of this book that it is impossible to mention them all.

The late Walter G. Klopfer, my friend and mentor, and for twenty-five years editor of the *Journal of Personality Assessment*, provided me with a warm and enthusiastic introduction to projective tests. I owe much to Walt.

My graduate training at Duke University encouraged me to think and ask questions, and to search for better answers. This process was aided and abetted most by Harold Schiffman, my dissertation advisor, a man with boundless curiosity, creativity, and a gourmet's taste for intellectual quality. Herb Crovitz and Irwin Kremen were also special teachers. I thank Bob Carson for his openness in exploring issues in personality and for encouraging his students to do the same.

Many people have generously given their time to read various Early Memory manuscripts. I am especially in debt to Martin Book, Ken Feigenbaum, Cheryl Shea-Gelernter, Bonnie Greenberg, Bob Holmstrom, Jim Mosel, Dick Sava, and David Trachtenberg.

Lori Assadi, Lori Crisler, Lee Kerman, and Mary Stone have assisted in manuscript preparation. Linda Hale Tobey contributed some library research and editorial suggestions. Kathy Fain Swanstrom put everything together and assisted me with some much needed editing. Their diligence and dedication are deeply appreciated.

My mother has always been encouraging and supportive of this process, and I thank my daughters Alexis and Erika for being themselves and adding to my own rich store of good memories. Alexis helped to make the book a family project by contributing library research. I am also grateful to Ellyn Kay for her love, support, and many editorial suggestions!

Thank you one and all.

Earliest Childhood Memories

1

INTRODUCTION

> If there be memory ... it is with a view of utility.... The function of
> the body is not to store up recollections, but simply to choose ... the
> useful memory, that which may complete and illuminate the present
> situation with a view to ultimate action.
>
> Henry Bergson

Freud's discovery of the unconscious and his interpretive work with
dreams are seminal contributions of the twentieth century. Absent
Freud, it would be difficult to imagine the existence of the "talking
therapies" that we know today. Yet as important as the unconscious is—
and it is extremely important—it involves only a small aspect of memory
functioning. What have been the parallel advances in preconscious and
conscious memory as it pertains to personality? Despite our increasing
understanding of the mind, we know almost nothing about the relationship between personality and memory. As amazing as it may seem,
this is the first non-edited book to be written on early memories and
personality, and the first on personality and autobiographical memories.

It is difficult to conceptualize a psychology of the self without memory
serving as a foundation. How is a sense of self formed from memory?
How does it happen that two people can experience the same event and
remember it so differently? Is perception responsible? Or memory? Or
both? If both are responsible, what variables can help us to understand
this process?

This book will not provide definitive answers to these questions, but
it will introduce a structure and a theory by which these questions can

be addressed. If we wish to grapple with such questions, we must adopt a view of humans and personality. If we believe that the central issue in human functioning revolves around the gratification of instinctual drives (psychoanalysis), then early memories will be used to understand this process (see Chapter 2). If we believe that each individual is impelled by a fictive final goal (Adlerian theory), then early memories will be analyzed with this in mind (see Chapter 2). This book has adopted a different view—Cognitive-Perceptual theory (see Chapter 3)—and analyzes early memories in a manner consistent with this orientation (see Chapter 4). This is not to say that Cognitive-Perceptual theory is better than other theories of personality—only different. Subsequently, how early memories can be approached and what they can teach us will differ from other perspectives.

Cognitive-Perceptual theory is rooted in perception and memory. The major question addressed by this theory is: how do perceptions change? The key to understanding perceptual differences is understanding memory differences. That is, the structure and organization of long-term autobiographical memory should determine how the individual processes immediate experience. Perception is not random. It is purposeful and directed. Sensory experience is much too vast to process in its totality. Somehow we must identify what is important as we accommodate to the world and adapt to our cultural milieu. Since all information is not equally important, we have also learned to prioritize perceptual data. A gun in our immediate environment is more significant to most of us than a sling shot; the anger in a man's voice as he screams at a young woman trembling on the ground is more noteworthy than the impatient bleating of an automobile horn two blocks away. While much data is processed, precious little is spotlighted and remembered. Most is quickly forgotten.

Although it is intuitively obvious that perception is not random, it is not a trivial matter to analyze the contents of autobiographical memory and specify what rules are used. It is also intuitively obvious that, just as all sensory data from current perceptions is not equally important, all memories in long-term autobiographical memory are not equally important.

How can we separate the significant from the trivial in long-term memory? One approach is to generate a set of intrinsically significant categories, determine whether any memories exist for these categories, and, if so, ascertain what these memories look like. For example, any memories categorized as traumatic should be important if there are any memories stored in this category; experiences of being sexually abused should also be important. When such memories exist, one can analyze how the individual constructed those experiences, and these constructions, in turn, should provide important clues as to how the individual processes *present* experience. Although this approach has face validity, its major disadvantage is that the individual may not recall events that conform to such categories. What then?

The second strategy is counterintuitive. It involves using EMs to understand perceptual differences. Why use *early* memories? Consider the following task. Recall as much as you can from yesterday—what your day was like, what you did, your strongest feelings, the highlight of the day, and so on. Now do the same for the day before that. And the day before that. Most people will quickly forget the specific happenings of individual days after a period of one to two weeks, but they could—with effort—reconstruct the highlights from a given week or month as they went backward in time for the past year. As the recollective process continues from the past year to the year before, to the year before that, and so forth, the number of specific events recalled diminishes rapidly at first, and then levels off until approximately age eight, when it diminishes rapidly again. Most individuals recall a mere handful of memories—at most—for each year prior to the eighth birthday until, by age two or three or four, the flame of remembrance is extinguished completely (see Figure 1.1).

Let us now return to our previous question. It is generally accepted among researchers that memory function conforms to *adaptive principles*—or put another way, memory is purposeful and not random. If so, it follows that EMs also conform to the principle of adaptation. But the scattered early memories that remain available to us must be *especially* important because they are survivors. Why do these particular experiences remain from so many that have faded in the mists of time? As Adler (Ansbacher & Ansbacher, 1956) put it:

> [From] the incalculable number of impressions which meet an individual, he chooses to remember only those which he feels, however darkly, to have a bearing on his situation. Thus his memories represent his "Story of My Life"; a story he repeats to himself to warn him or comfort him, to keep him concentrated on his goal, and to prepare him by means of past experiences, so that he will meet the future with an already tested style of action. (p. 351)

In other words, the material that appears in EMs is chosen due to its *present* relevance. It reflects how we see things *now*. It is the *continuity* between our understanding of our present situation and our remembrance of the past that determines which memories emerge from the recesses of childhood experience.

Figure 1.1
The Hypothesized Frequency of Specific Recollections for Male College Students by Age of Occurrence

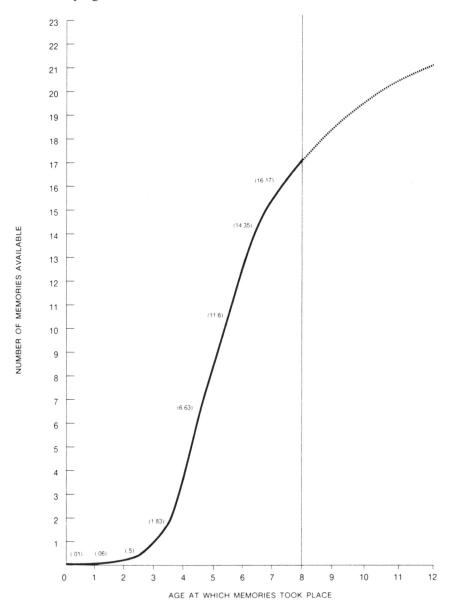

_____ : Drawn after Waldfogel (1948) for male college Ss

.... : Hypothesized extention of curve

ARE EARLY MEMORIES "MEMORIES"?

From one point of view, most EMs are not memories at all. Most are creatively constructed fantasies about the past that reveal present attitudes and mood as well as issues that are unresolved for the individual. That these "memories" are fantasies, and not actual memories, was convincingly demonstrated by Mayman (1968/1984a):

> It is, in fact, possible to demonstrate that virtually all early memories, which are so blithely taken for granted, could not have been experienced in the form in which they are remembered. One need only carry out a fairly simple inquiry. If one asks whether the memory occurs as a scene one imagines visually, the answer is almost always yes. If one then asks whether the informant appears as one of the figures in that scene, one learns that in more than half of all early memories the person *sees* himself as a little child as if he, the child, were another person and he, the observer, were looking on from some point away from the center of action. Moreover, the scene is often viewed from above, or from outside a window looking in, or from some other equally unlikely or impossible vantage point. One can imagine the event in that way, but surely the scene was never experienced that way in actuality. The memory is a *reconstruction* of a real or fantasied event rather than the re-experiencing of a *living* event. Even in those less common memories where the person says he *feels* himself to be present, and sees the scene as if from where he was standing at the time, one need only ask him from what eye-level he sees the people and things around him and how large they appear, to determine once again that he does not experience that scene as he would have at the age when the event is said to have occurred; he visualizes the setting as it would appear to him at an older age, or perhaps even as he would now view them as an adult. (p. 127)

Mayman notes that "more than half of all early memories" are fantasies in which the individual re-experiences the memory as an outside observer. In my experience with individuals seen clinically, ninety-five percent is perhaps a more realistic estimate of the percentage of fantasy memories—and this estimate is likely to be conservative.

What about the miniscule minority of EMs that appear to represent the event as it was experienced at that time? These appear to be true early *memories*—not fantasies, but actual recollections. They are extremely rare, but they do exist. I obtained several from one client that dated from the first two years of life, including one from his first year in which the client recalled a surgical repair of a botched circumcision.

He remembered the doctor's telling his mother that the procedure would be done under local anesthetic because an infant that age could not feel the scalpel. The client vividly recalled the initial shock that he felt and the pain afterwards. The accuracy of the memory was confirmed in a taped interview with the client's mother. The two of them had apparently never discussed the memory before, and the mother was amazed that her son could remember the incident. In this particular case, although the client appeared to re-experience the event exactly as it occurred at the time, *the same principles of interpretation are applicable*, whether the memory was a fantasy or a reliving of an early experience.

Two more examples are provided by Milton Erickson, the eminent hypnotherapist, from his own recollections. These memories, which are reported by Gordon and Meyers-Anderson (1981), date to his first fifteen months of life:

> When I first went to college, I got interested in memories. I thought it over carefully: how soon would there be enough learning by an infant to permit memories? And what kind of memories would they be? Now I recall my first spanking at the age of nine months. And I wrote it out in detail and when I went back to the farm, I asked my parents if there had been another cabin in the Sierra Nevada Mountains. They said, "Yes, the cabin we used to live in was way down the valley . . . several miles away there was another cabin." Mother and Father thought it over and finally recalled that they had made a visit there. And I said, "You wore long dresses then and you sat on a chair and I saw Mrs. Cameron pick up something and put it somewhere and it made a beautiful splash of color. So I crept over, took something and put it there and made a beautiful splash of color and Mrs. Cameron, only I didn't know her name, spanked me. I was enraged. I crept up to my mother's chair and hid behind her skirts." My mother and father recalled, "Oh yes, you threw something in the fireplace at the Cameron cabin and Mrs. Cameron picked you up and spanked you and explained, 'When a child is wrong, you spank him right away.' " I still feel that horrible sense of outrage—why could [*sic*] [would?] she put something there?—I get spanked for it! It was just plain outrageous!
>
> My next memory was there were two objects triangular in shape. I subsequently realized that they were women. And they were showing me a Christmas tree with a lighted candle on it. And in the background there was a two legged thing with a lot of hair on its face. I asked my parents if there had been a Christmas tree? They agreed, "Yes there had been," but they couldn't remember that particular Christmas and the questions came down to dating that memory. And that memory was finally identified as December 25th,

1902. I was one year and three weeks old. And my parents dated that memory because that hairy-faced man was my father trying on an outfit for my mother and sister. And my parents dated it by working out when my father shaved off his beard. And in February 1903 my father told my mother, "I'm tired of the boy grabbing my whiskers to pull himself up." So they clearly identified the memory. Those two peculiar triangular objects and that two legged creature with a lot of hair on its face . . . when you give yourself permission to remember things it is astonishing because we all have the attitude, "Oh that was kid stuff." Kid stuff is very important, it is the background for knowing things. (pp. 165, 166)

It is remarkable that Erickson's first EMs date to ages nine months and one year and three months, which is unusually early. Although it is difficult to prove beyond a reasonable doubt that these are recollections of events as they actually occurred—and not reworked fantasies about such events—several elements suggest that Erickson had re-experienced the events as he described. Erickson, in the first EM: (1) recalled behaving as a nine-month-old would (e.g., he "crept over" and imitated what Mrs. Cameron had done); (2) remembered that his mother wore a long dress then, suggesting that he could see the scene; and (3) re-experienced his original feeling at the time—rage. In addition, Erickson's parents supplied Mrs. Cameron's statements, which Erickson was unlikely to process at his age, the more so after he became enraged when being spanked. His second EM also contains two elements that suggest he re-experienced what he reported: (1) he recalled the people as shapes ("two objects triangular in shape"), suggesting that the material had not be reworked (else he would immediately describe them as "my mother and sister"); (2) he remembered his father as a "two legged thing with a lot of hair on its face"—a description consistent with what an infant's recollection might be. He did not, for instance, recall the incident as his "father trying on an outfit for my mother and sister," which would have required reprocessing in order to describe the scene from a more advanced developmental perspective. Extremely early recollections of the type that Erickson reports must, by their very nature, be *confusing as originally experienced* because infants and toddlers *lack the sophistication in their schemas* to describe something that happened to them as they would if they were adults looking back at the scene. I tend to believe that Erickson describes his EMs much as they were experienced at the time.

In a sense, the term EMs is a *misnomer*. Perhaps EMs should be described as "Fantasized Events Attributed to Early Childhood"—FEAECs. Such a description has the merit of representing the phenomenon of EMs more accurately. Unfortunately, this phrase—while accurate—is not something that most of us would accept because we experience our EMs at a visceral level as *historical truths* and resist conceptualizing them as period fantasies or historical fictions.

Unlike Erickson's EMs, most EMs function as fantasy material. An example is provided below. As her comments suggest, the client is aware of her need for autonomy and her tremendous aversion to being controlled:

> EM1. Is me on a summer day sitting out in a playpen. I can see me in a playpen. It has been used before—on one side, there was a missing rung that had been repaired with a piece of string, or rope, and I can see me coming through the playpen. In some way I undid the rope, and I was free of the playpen. I was about two or two and a half-years old. (What is clearest in the memory?) I see exactly how I got out of it. But I can see me sitting inside with the baby bottle and blanket. (What is the strongest feeling in the memory?) Feeling of wanting to be free—not wanting to be in there. (How does the memory end?) I can recall getting out and running down the street. I can see myself just being free. I don't remember what direction I went. But I do remember being free—of my own volition.

The fantasy nature of this memory is evident in several respects. The most convincing is that the client sees herself in the playpen as an observer would—an obvious impossibility if she were reliving this episode. As has been estimated, fully 95 percent or more of a random clinical population report fantasy EMs. The Milton Erickson type of EM rarely appears. Thus, with a few exceptions, EMs can be viewed as fantasies and interpreted as projective data. But even when EMs describe real events as they actually occurred, they can be interpreted as if they were fantasies, just as Erickson's first EM reflects issues with injustice and being controlled (he was punished for something that he wanted to do).

THE ORGANIZATION OF AUTOBIOGRAPHICAL MEMORY

Cognitive-Perceptual theory holds that autobiographical memory contains a potpourri of memories that can be likened to metal filings. Some memories are analogous to pure iron. Some are like iron comingled with other metals. Some are non-ferrous entirely—such as pure copper. By the *principle of attraction*, that which is recalled from long-term memory is pulled by the magnet of present-day interests, attitudes, expectations, and perceptions. We recall from long-term memory what is *today* consistent with our most strongly held attitudes, perceptions, and expectations. Our reconstruction of early childhood experiences is not only consistent with our present beliefs, but how we recall these events reinforces what we believe today. For instance, if we believe that others will victimize us if given an opportunity, we will recall events that support this belief and use these experiences to justify our perception of others. If we wish to understand how autobiographical memory is organized for a particular individual, we must examine its products. This topic will be discussed in greater detail in Chapter 3.

THE FIRST EARLY MEMORY—IS IT SPECIAL?

The first EM is considered special by many writers, particularly some Adlerians. Adler (1931) himself raised EMs as a group to a place of special prominence. He held that an individual's EMs are:

> the reminders he carries about with him of his own limits and of the meaning of circumstances. . . . [They serve as] a story he repeats to himself to warn him or comfort him, to keep him concentrated on his goal, to prepare him, by means of past experiences, to meet the future with an already tested style of action. (p. 73)

Although he valued early memories, it is unclear from the preceding (which is often quoted in the literature) whether Adler believed that the first memory was particularly important. After a period of confusion in the literature, Alder's biographer, Ansbacher (1953), interpreted Adler's position to be that all EMs—both first and later memories—were special because they revealed the "individual's style of life." Ansbacher was correct for I recently happened upon a statement from Adler (1929) that spoke directly to this point:

> From the endless store of childhood memories which each one of us has, only a few are carried over into maturity. This very fact should emphasize the importance of these remembered impressions. And so when an adult tells us of an early remembrance (it matters little whether it is the first or not) which is particularly clear to him, we are able to interpret from it the speaker's personal attitude toward life. (p. 6)

Adler's personal belief aside, the question remains open as to whether the first EM is special in some way. I believe that it is. The basis for its special status can be understood from three different arguments. The first is partly circular but deserves mention nonetheless. The first memory is the ultimate survivor—the earliest remnant from millions of early experiences. As such, it is reasonable to suppose that there must be something special about this particular experience, for it survived while others receded into the mists of antiquity.

The second argument proceeds from the nature of memory. It is well established that memory is organized to conform to the principle of *utility*. We remember what we do for a reason: the data is useful to us. That which is not useful is discarded. Since EMs conform to this principle, we can hypothesize that the *longer* information remains with us, the more important it must be. In the case of our first memory, any recollection of such great antiquity must have particular utility in order for it to survive so long.

The third argument considers the role of the first memory in a series of EMs. The first EM serves as the psychological *anchorpoint* in a series of EMs and ordinarily causes other EMs to be recalled *by association*. Something about the first memory *triggers* subsequent EMs. For most individuals, subsequent EMs become *elaborations* on the main theme(s) introduced in the first EM. If the first EM focuses on a loss, for example, there is a high probability that subsequent EMs will describe other losses (e.g., a death, a family move, the parents' divorce).

It makes sense to believe that the first memory is special. But whether the first memory has particular efficacy as a diagnostic tool, and whether it is more revealing than other EMs are questions that must be tested by research. Some tentative answers to these questions will appear in the review of the literature in Volume II.

UNFINISHED BUSINESS IN EARLY MEMORIES

What do we know about the character of memory that will permit us to understand how autobiographical memory is organized? If a researcher were to ask a college sophomore to remember the random digit series, 6–2–4–3–7–1–9, the student might recall it for several minutes before forgetting it. But if the student is told that the string of digits is the telephone number of someone whom he has wanted to meet, he may recall this number indefinitely. We remember what is important to us and forget the rest.

This example provides a clue as to how autobiographical memory must be organized. If it is true that we remember what is important, it can be demonstrated by inequalities in forgetting that all things initially remembered are not equally important. The principle of first among equals must operate in memory, or autobiographical memory would be hopelessly cluttered with information. Our own life experience tells us there must be hierarchical organization. If so, what principles determine priority?

One variable that determines priority—and thus availability of information—in autobiographical memory can be conceptualized as *issues in process*. To understand this concept, consider a typical day in your life. You awaken with an agenda in mind—drop off the car for a brake job, get the analysis on the Smith deal to the boss, work up the numbers for the building lease for Eddy, and confirm reservations at the restaurant for dinner tonight. Without some kind of daily agenda, whether sketchy or highly detailed, we would never get out of bed in the morning. By analogy, autobiographical memory follows a similar organizational scheme that we use in our daily lives. Certain matters are deemed to be important, and these matters receive disproportionate attention in autobiographical memory. This does not necessarily mean that we are consciously aware of what these issues are, any more than we can specify at 6:00 A.M. what our priorities are for the day. Sometimes we can, and other times we cannot. Sometimes the priorities make themselves known as the day evolves. But the priorities that determine recall exist in autobiographical memory whether or not we are consciously aware of them. This set of priorities determines our selection of early memories from our childhood.

When we talk about issues in process, we are referring to what important tasks need to be done, or *what is unfinished in our lives*. In most cases, the major issues evident in autobiographical memory are relatively few in number. There is a reason for this. For the same reason we do not clutter our daily agendas with low priority tasks we know we do not have time to undertake, we do not burden autobiographical memory with an excessive number of issues we do not have the time or skills to resolve. We must also keep in mind an intrinsic problem associated with the nature of issues that we work on—the *interdependence* of these issues. For instance, working on emotional intimacy may be of prime importance to us. But if we cannot assert ourselves or self-disclose, intimacy may be an impossible goal to achieve. Resolving a higher-level issue may first require working through a nested set of interdependent, lower-level issues, just as developing assertiveness skills and an ability to self-disclose are necessary before emotional intimacy can be attained.

The relationship between unresolved issues and EMs is straightforward. We remember what is important. The most important recollections are then distinguished from the less important on an ongoing basis and given priority in autobiographical memory. It is this material that is readily available to consciousness. These memories reflect our current view of life and our current issues in process. Just as autobiographical memory as a whole gives weight to such memories, so also do EMs, which are but a subset of autobiographical memory.

That EMs deal with matters that are unresolved is supported by the following argument. Assume that EMs reference only matters that are resolved. If so, recalling such memories would be like making a daily agenda of those things that we have already done. Such an organizational scheme would not be adaptive and, in fact, is contrary to everything that we know about human nature. It is adaptive to focus on what most needs to be done, and this is how autobiographical memory is organized—to remind us via specific recollections of what is most pressing in our personal development. Some EMs—positive affect EMs—deal with partly or wholly resolved issues, but these are relatively uncommon. This topic will be explored in Chapter 5.

EARLY MEMORIES: A PRELIMINARY DEFINITION

It is a simple matter to provide a preliminary definition of an EM. Unfortunately, there are instances in which this definition needs to be modified. These matters will be discussed further in Chapter 5 and in Volume II.

For now, let us define an EM as follows: A recollection of a specific, one-time childhood event of the form, "I remember one time..." The EM ordinarily describes an event that occurred before an individual's eighth birthday.

This definition works well in many cases, but it is too simple. Several pragmatic considerations, which will be raised later, require a more detailed definition. For instance, what if the memory pertains to an incident that was told to the individual, not something that he himself recalls? What if we are working with a population of six-or seven-year-old children or with adults in their eighties? Perhaps the eighth birthday needs to be used as a guideline rather than as an invariant rule. And what about events that occurred more than one time, such as "We always used to have a picnic at my grandmother's after Sunday church when I was little." If these are not EMs, what are they, and how should they be treated for clinical and research purposes? These matters will be addressed in Volume II when methodological issues are discussed.

THEORIES OF PERSONALITY AND COGNITIVE-PERCEPTUAL THEORY

If anything, an individual is complex and can be viewed from many perspectives like a many-faceted gem. Since no one perspective reveals the whole picture, something can be learned from each viewpoint.

What are some of the ways that personality can be conceptualized? One can argue that if personality can be reduced to a series of learned events, personality can be conceptualized in terms of what we have learned and how. If so, *social learning theory* is the result. Alternatively, we could argue that personality is mostly genetically predetermined and that learning is irrelevant for the most part. If so, a personality theory based on *temperament* or genetics would result. We could conceptualize a person as an organism whose actions are motivated mainly by attempts to satisfy instinctual drives while at the same time minimizing problems for himself. If so, Freudian theory would be the result. A distinctly different approach is to study behavior and to attempt to understand what goals motivate the individual to act. Examples of this approach would be Lewin's Field Theory and Adler's Individual Psychology. Others have conceptualized personality as a complex network of needs that vary in kind and strength by individual. Human behavior can thus be perceived as organized to satisfy these needs. As the preceding examples demonstrate, we can conceptualize personality from many perspectives. No one point of view will reveal everything that we want to know, but each will provide its unique insights.

Just as people can be viewed through many different personality theories, so also can EMs and autobiographical memories be analyzed. The literature now contains a classical psychoanalytic view of EMs, an ego-psychological approach to EMs, and an Adlerian perspective on EMs (see Chapter 2). We can also imagine other theoretical approaches, which have not as yet been described, just as many approaches to personality exist.

While still in graduate school, I was struck by the fact that there was no theory of personality based on *memory* and, similarly, no model of EM interpretation grounded on memory principles. With this in mind, an early version of Cognitive-Perceptual theory began to take shape in the mid–1970s. Several critical questions emerged in the development of this theory. The first was how to conceptualize memory, as many choices were possible. I decided to return to Bartlett's (1932) classical work on memory. Bartlett conceptualized memory as conforming to principles of *utility* (we remember what is useful) and *adaptation* (we remember what makes us more adaptable, in a Darwinian sense). The next issue was the orientation of this theory: what is it intended to explain? I designed it to account for personality change. The next problem was to describe what happens to autobiographical memory when personality change occurs. From a Cognitive-Perceptual perspective, personality change can be considered as a qualitative change in thinking, marked by a change in expectations, attitudes, perceptions, and ultimately, behaviors. When thinking changes qualitatively, behavior begins to change consistent with changes in thought process. If the personality change reflects a higher level of adaptation, behavior becomes more adaptive, and needs that were previously frustrated can now be satisfied. Of course, the reverse is true also—an individual may regress and lose skills and insights as he adopts maladaptive attitudes.

This volume will concentrate primarily on the application of the Cognitive-Perceptual method to the interpretation of EMs and autobiographical memories. Illustrations of how Cognitive-Perceptual theory can also be applied to the process of psychotherapy will be given in Volume II.

BELIEF AND REALITY

Many psychologists regard autobiographical memories as historical truths and thus find it impossible to conceive of memories as projective data. Cognitive-Perceptual theory holds that a knowledge of historical reality is less important in understanding an individual than the manner in which the individual chooses to interpret that reality. The reconstruction of the past is determined by the current belief system, which is composed of a network of basic axioms (attitudes) about the world. As will be seen in Chapter 4, many of the early experiences of Golda Meir (former Prime Minister of Israel) would have devastated another personality. But Meir used what many would have experienced as traumatic events to energize herself to work to make Israel stronger. Thus, it was not her past experiences, but how she chose to interpret those experiences, that was critical in developing her world view.

To illustrate the constructive process, consider an individual who remembers a childhood incident in which his mother yelled at him. We will assume that the event actually occurred. How can this incident be constructed? Many possibilities come to mind, including:

1. Mother didn't love me, and that's why she yelled at me.
2. Mother was always mean to me—she never yelled at the others.
3. Mother loved me a lot, but her temper was set on a short fuse, and when she became angry she blew up at whomever or whatever was handy.
4. Mother depended on me a lot, and when I let her down she became upset with me and yelled.
5. Mother was a perfectionist, and when people made mistakes she had little tolerance.

Other constructions are possible, including "I could never make her happy," or "The incident stands out for its uniqueness," and so forth. Constructions may focus on attitudes involving the self, another, a situation ("After my father died, this was a very stressful period in our lives"), or some combination of the three.

In the law, attorneys are sometimes known to say, "The facts speak for themselves." When working with autobiographical memories, we may instead rely on the following axiom: The facts rarely speak for themselves. An individual's interpretation of the facts is what is important. In the grand scheme of things, reality counts, but it counts far less than our interpretation of reality.

Let us next consider one of the most fundamental aspects of a belief system—attitudes involving the self. This part of a belief system exerts an enormous pull on how an individual interprets past and present events. The following example of a male college student is given as a case in point:

Fact about the self: I am below average in attractiveness (accepted as true for illustrative purposes).

Hypothetical Beliefs Related to This Fact:

1. Because I am unattractive, no one will be interested in me.
2. Because I am unattractive, I am doomed to be a failure in life.
3. Because I am unattractive, I will have to work harder than others to prove my worth.
4. I may be unattractive, but at least I can improve my physical appearance by diet and exercise (to be the best that I can be).
5. I may be less attractive than others, but I will work on making myself more appealing in other ways—for example, I will become more empathetic, learn to listen better, make others laugh.

As the preceding example indicates, the individual may construct the fact of being unattractive in a number of ways. How this is done is a matter of personal choice. That we adopt a personal belief system is a critical presupposition in all psychotherapy systems that value insight and seek to foster it. For instance, an insight-oriented psychotherapist must hold his client accountable for his beliefs ("Your mother represented your father as cold and unloving, and you chose to buy into her beliefs.") In order for change to occur, an insight-oriented therapist must hold his client accountable for how he has chosen to construct reality.

The theoretical discussion in Chapter 3 will contain an elaboration of these ideas. How maladaptive attitudes can be approached in therapy will be discussed in Volume II.

MALADAPTIVE ATTITUDES AND AUTOBIOGRAPHICAL MEMORY

From a clinical perspective, an important goal of the Cognitive-Perceptual method is to identify maladaptive attitudes in autobiographical memory. Once a maladaptive attitude is identified, the therapist seeks to develop a strategy for challenging that attitude and helping the client replace it with something more adaptive.

What is a maladaptive attitude? As used in Cognitive-Perceptual theory, a maladaptive attitude is a belief that impedes or blocks the satisfaction of needs or the attainment of goals that the individual consciously wants to reach. The clinical example given in the Preface will serve as a convenient illustration. In this case, the client viewed himself as unlovable, which left him with a damaged sense of self and a low-grade depression. This attitude appeared to be derived from the client's construction of his relationship with his mother. In an EM that summarized the more salient aspects of this relationship, he recalled the disapproval on his mother's face as she berated him for some long-forgotten, minor misdeed. The maladaptive attitude rooted in this memory is the client's belief that he was unlovable, which was acted out in his interaction with his mother. His mother was yelling at him for something, and he recalled feeling ashamed and worthless. The therapist chose to work on the maladaptive attitude by attempting to graft onto the EM a more benign interpretation—that although his mother did in fact yell at him, she loved him nevertheless. When a critical attitude ("I am not lovable") that has assumed axiomatic proportions in the personality organization is replaced, dramatic personality changes can follow.

Autobiographical memories, with their rich metaphorical character, provide an easy entree into the individual's phenomenological world— how he or she views the world and why. Once the individual's construction of critical paradigmatic events in his life is understood from an analysis of his autobiographical memories ("When others get upset with me, I feel worthless"), the clinician is better able to identify the problem and begin to resolve it.

THE UNIQUENESS OF AUTOBIOGRAPHICAL MEMORIES AS AN ASSESSMENT TECHNIQUE

The self is as the self remembers. To the extent that we want to explore the organization of the self—its major needs, perceptions, and major unresolved issues—there is no more efficient method than an analysis of autobiographical memories. As will be shown in Chapters 3, 4, and 5, that information which is most relevant to present perceptions is contained in autobiographical memory and can be readily accessed through the Early Memories Procedure (see Chapter 5).

Although many projective tests of autobiographical memory can be imagined, none exists save for EMs (Chapters 2, 3, and 4) and the *Early Memories Procedure* (Chapter 5).[1] Given the centrality of the self to personality assessment, it is truly astounding that a test of autobiographical memory was not formulated earlier. Perhaps the closest previous approximation to a test of autobiographical memory is word association tests, which are ill-suited to understanding the complexities of intrapsychic conflicts. Sometimes word association tests tap attitudes imbedded in early autobiographical memories, but they are just as likely to pull data from other sources. Consider the following probe/association: "mother"—"cold." This response may derive from several early, vivid, affect-laden memories in autobiographical memory, or it may originate, for instance, from feelings associated with the recent breakup of a romantic relationship that have spilled over into the individual's good feelings about his mother (as if to say, "all women are cold, therefore mothers are cold"). The point is that it is never clear just from the response itself what may prompt a particular association. The *Early Memories Procedure* does not bypass this problem entirely, but it minimizes it.

I have encountered considerable confusion from professionals when I ask them how they assess autobiographical memory. A typical example is a clinician who responded, "I suppose I do what most clinicians do: early in the intake session I say, 'Tell me about yourself,' and that usually gives me a good overview." Unfortunately, probes such as "Tell me about yourself" do *not* tap autobiographical memory. They assess the individual's *historical record*, which is not composed of memories per se, but of a summary of aspects of one's life believed to have interest to others in one's culture. For instance, when most Americans are asked such a question, they will talk briefly about when and where they were born, their parents, how many siblings they had, where they grew up, what schools they attended and graduated from, and so on. In many respects, one can conceptualize the historical record as something like a newspaper obituary—facts that we think others might want to know about us. However, the historical record rarely contains specific EMs, but rather basic historical facts and summaries of epochs or aspects of our lives ("I have worked for several large firms as a programmer involved with direct-mail marketing projects"). After discussing the assessment of autobiographical memory with many professionals, I strongly suspect that the majority of clinicians do not make any systematic assessment of autobiographical memory.

The classical projective tests—the Rorschach and TAT—appear to tap autobiographical memory *indirectly*. That is, the cards stimulate responses that are derived from the same wishes, impulses, needs, attitudes, and so on, that determine the selection of EMs and other autobiographical memories. To understand the individual's responses, however, one must also understand the meaning of the stimulus to the individual (the "stimulus pull"), which may also have socio-cultural aspects. Moreover, there is the problem of where the test is given (jail, school), how the testing room is decorated (warm, austere), the gender of the examiner and the testee's past history with this gender as an authority figure, how the examiner presents himself (friendly, neutral, distant), and so forth. Research suggests that both instruments are highly sensitive to a wide variety of subtle influences. As a result, responses can be significantly influenced by transient factors in the environment. As will be discussed further in Volume II, EMs tend to be much more stable, especially in content, suggesting a resistance to transient, short-term effects.

Early memories are highly stable for most individuals and tend to remain constant in terms of basic thematic structure unless significant personality growth or change takes place, as one might find in psychotherapy clients (see Volume II), or individuals who are experiencing significant life changes. Moreover, EMs tend to deal with the big picture in personality—what Mosak (1958) called *the headlines*. Thus, EMs play out major issues, not transient minor concerns that must be factored out of an individual's test protocol. It is this summarizing—or orienting—function of EMs that makes them particularly valuable as a projective device.

CONTEXT AND DEFENSE

So often in psychological reports, one finds phrases such as, "The client appears to experience difficulty managing his aggressive impulses." What does this mean? That he is a walking time bomb ready to detonate at any moment or that under certain circumstances he may act aggressively toward others?

The difference between these concepts is the difference between a *mechanistic theory* of personality that conceptualizes human functioning as the complex interplay between drive and defense and a *contextual theory* (Cognitive-Perceptual theory) that perceives human functioning as oriented toward resolving critical problems so that growth can take place. Classical psychoanalytic theory, as proposed by Freud, is a mechanistic system that follows a hydraulic model (e.g., drives may "build up" and "overwhelm" defenses designed to "contain" them).

A mechanistic model can be effectively used to understand behavior in the case of certain drives—hunger for instance—but whether an aggressive drive exists is open to question. I have observed many *Early Memories Procedure* (EMP) protocols that reflect high power and aggression needs, but whether these needs also exist as drives, comparable to the hunger drive, is debatable. To date, I am not aware that the existence of an aggressive drive in humans has been biologically demonstrated.

In any event, psychoanalytic theory as a mechanistic model proposes that we all come equipped with the same basic drives, and we all must negotiate the same psychosexual stages of development. In other words, people are very much alike—it is the variety and sophistication of our defenses that distinguishes us. Similarly, psychoanalysis does not aim to resolve a conflict so much as to manage it more effectively through the use of higher level defenses.

On the other hand, Cognitive-Perceptual theory focuses specifically on growth and change and how such takes place. The model is set up to facilitate an understanding of an individual's issues in process and, ultimately, how to resolve them.

With this theoretical material as background, let us return to our discussion of mechanistic versus contextual perspectives on aggression. Two EM case studies will be used as illustrations. The first involves an adolescent boy who was referred for an evaluation following his arrest for kidnapping a neighbor boy. The client threatened the victim with a gun and martial arts weapons and stomped him when he resisted his orders. The client's EMs began with a violent and aggressive memory in which he was the victim of his father's aggression and ended with memories in which he was the aggressor. Relating this set of memories agitated the client so much that he began pacing from one end of the office to the other and punctuating his remarks with martial arts kicks and blows to the air as we "talked." This was an extremely aggressive, dangerous young man. Since he had been victimized and brutalized by his father, he perceived two roles in human relationships: You either dominate and "kick butt," or others dominate and brutalize you. This was his world view: Life is a jungle, and only the strongest survive.

In the second case, an adolescent reported a number of EMs of accidental injuries. Although these memories conveyed a sense of vulnerability and fragility, they concluded with *afterthoughts* (see Chapter 4) that emphasized how he had battled to regain functioning that had been lost as a result of these injuries. The overall theme was, "I may get hurt, but I'll never give up." Several of the injuries were sustained while he was involved in competitive team sports. His last memory, however, involved his mother's being beaten by his stepfather, a fairly regular event in his family life. After watching such incidents helplessly in his younger years, he finally decided that enough was enough. A martial arts student, he told his stepfather to let his mother alone. The stepfather said something demeaning to the boy and then took a swing at him. The boy avoided the punch and knocked him out with a single punch. End of fight. The sequence of memories, with the fight memory at the end, suggested that issues involving aggression were not prominent in his life. However, feelings of vulnerability were. By history, this was a youngster with pacifist beliefs who abhorred the use of violence in settling disputes. There were no prior incidents of aggression whatsoever, aside from the altercation with his stepfather. Several years after he was first evaluated, he, by chance, happened upon a couple involved in an argument. As he arrived, the man struck the woman with his fist, knocking her down.

The young man interceded, saying, "Look, calm down and talk this over. I'm sure that you can work this out." Apparently not given to negotiation, the man threw a punch at this voice of reason, who in turn aimed a well-timed blow to the man's chin. End of fight.

What do we make of the preceding incident? Early memories specify not only which issues are salient, *but also the context in which these issues are likely to be evoked.* The context of the couple fighting—something that most people would have avoided—attracted him. He tried to intercede and resolve the situation peaceably—just as he likely wanted to do in years past when his stepfather and mother fought. But when he was attacked, he responded exactly as he had with his stepfather. It was a particular context—a couple fighting and a woman being hit—that pulled him into the conflict and eventually elicited an aggressive response.

In sum, a set of EMs can provide pertinent information on the following variables: the issue, the particular context that is likely to evoke the issue, and the degree to which the individual is defended if the issue involves impulse control. In the first case, the adolescent was presented as extremely aggressive and very dangerous. His world view was that one either dominates or one will be dominated and victimized. Every memory had the same form, except that he was the victim in his earlier memories. His memories suggested that little or nothing was required to provoke aggressive incidents—they just happened. Therefore, a need to contain aggressive impulses was unnecessary. In the second case, by contrast, management of aggressive impulses was a minor issue. Only one aggressive memory was given, it was placed at the end of a series of memories, and the individual was attacked before he retaliated. This individual appeared to be distressed by aggressive behavior and preferred to function in the role of peacemaker or, alternatively, the rescuer of damsels in distress. This failing, he defended himself to the extent needed to blunt the aggression of others.

EARLY MEMORIES AS REAL EVENTS

How accurate is autobiographical memory? Can EMs be validated as having occurred? If an EM actually occurred, does this mean that it caused the individual to become what he is today? These are important questions. Let us consider each in turn.

Questions pertaining to the accuracy of autobiographical memories fall largely outside the purview of this book. Of course, it would be interesting to know the extent to which a recollection was accurate. It would also be interesting to demonstrate the kinds of variables that induce distortions in memories over time. This book—and especially Cognitive-Perceptual theory—is mostly concerned with the sequelae of any distortional process that might be operative, as opposed to the process by which the material is distorted. Genetic psychology, on the other hand, tends to regard memories as factual data and works with memories in this fashion (see Volume II). In contrast to genetic psychology, Cognitive-Perceptual theory views EMs as fantasies about the past that reveal present perceptions, interests, and concerns, as well as unfinished business in process. This statement should not be taken to mean that all EMs are pure myths. Some EMs are myths, and others are quite distorted. Others happen to be more or less accurate as stated. But whether true or false, partly true or partly false, all EMs are selected to reveal present perceptions, interests, concerns, and issues in process.

A comment regarding determinism is also relevant here. Several humanistically oriented professors were so offended by my proposed dissertation study on EMs that they refused to sit on my committee lest their actions be construed as supporting Freudian determinism! Nor did their objection reflect a misinterpretation of Freud (1905/1938), who wrote: "We must assume ... that the very impressions which we have forgotten [i.e., early childhood experiences] have nevertheless left the deepest traces in psychic life, and acted as determinants for our whole future development" (pp. 581–582). Freud is certainly correct in principle. We are profoundly influenced by early experience. However, there are some problems in logic with respect to how some Freudians approach EMs. Many Freudians reason thusly: Early experience determines future development; EMs comprise a partial historical record of this early experience; therefore, EMs depict the occurrence of incidents that determined future development. This logic fails on two counts: (1) the early experiences that did in fact influence us to become who we are today are not necessarily the subject of our EMs; (2) EMs are not necessarily accurate historically. Only when we recognize that EMs are creatively selected to reflect how we perceive things now can we appreciate that the issue of determinism is largely onthogonal to a discussion of EMs.

Let us next consider in Chapter 2 the EM models that predated Cognitive-Perceptual theory. These include the Freudian, Adlerian, and ego-psychological models.

NOTE

1. A second test of autobiographical memory that assesses attitudes associated with romantic relationships has recently been published—Bruhn, A. R. (1990) *The Romantic Relationships Procedure*. Bethesda, MD: Psychline Press.

2

THE PREDECESSORS OF COGNITIVE-PERCEPTUAL THEORY

The neurotic does not suffer from his reminiscences, he makes them
... and uses them for his purposes.

Alfred Adler

Any new theory owes much to its predecessors. So it is with Cognitive-Perceptual theory (see Chapter 3). In this chapter, we will review the predecessors of Cognitive-Perceptual theory. Each theory has contributed to it, and each has value as a separate and distinct method of interpreting EMs.[1]

Early memory theory dates from 1899 with some brief comments by Freud about screen memories. Freud continued to elaborate a psychoanalytic theory of early memories in subsequent papers. As best as I can determine, Adler first began to discuss EMs in 1912. Ego psychologists incorporated aspects of both positions starting in the 1950s.

FREUD'S VIEW OF EMs

Freud's thinking regarding EMs is closely connected with his theory of infantile amnesia (S. Freud, 1916/1971). In brief, he postulated that at the close of the Oedipal phase of development, as the child enters latency, a great portion of childhood experience falls under a "shroud of oblivion" (p. 210). A major task in the latency period is the repression of the incestuous and murderous fantasies directed toward parents and siblings. This repression is necessary, from an adaptive point of view, to free the child's energy for further cognitive development and sublimatory activities during the latency period. The few memories that re-main from the Oedipal period are distorted and disguised to protect the child from becoming upset by their content. Freud (1899/1950) noted that memories from the Oedipal period are manifestly concerned with everyday events yet are surprisingly rich in detail. He coined the term "screen memories" for this phenomenon.

Freud (1899/1950) found screen memories to be quite common among the individuals he treated. As he investigated the apparent blandness of these memories, he found instead material that helped to elucidate the infantile conflicts of his patients. Kennedy (1950) provided an example of a screen memory in her discussion of a latency-aged girl's recollection of her fourth year. Kennedy was fortunate in that the girl had lived with her between the ages of nine months and five years. The EM was as follows: "Once I kept on playing the piano and you told me to stop, but I continued and you got very angry with me." Kennedy noted the event never took place and discussed the EM in terms of the child's difficulty in managing instinctual urges, particularly around toilet training.

Freud (1916/1971) likened the production of screen memories to the process of symptom formation (see also Greenacre, 1952). Screen mem-ories were viewed as a compromise that ensues from a conflict between an unconscious forbidden wish and a defense against that wish. The result is a distorted product that reflects both forces. By a process of free association, Freud was able to discover the latent meaning of the memory.

Original analytic thinking (e.g., S. Freud, 1899/1950, 1901/1960, 1917/1955) clearly suggests that once the distortions and displacement of the screen memory are analyzed, one will discover the memory of an actual occurrence, which will often relate to something sexual. More recent papers (e.g., A. Freud, 1951; Kennedy, 1971; Kris, 1956b) argue instead that EMs most often reflect whole periods of development condensed into a single "event." Consistent with Kris' (1956b) warning against the search "to find the 'events' of the afternoon on the staircase when the seduction happened" (p. 73), Kennedy (1971) advises therapists to view the EM as a child's unique perception of the external world and not a report of actual events. In either case, for Freudians, the EM is a product of and about the past which is retained in the present. Significant dis-tortions may occur, but the clinician views the EMs as an historical artifact.

ADLER'S VIEW OF EMs

Adler's view of EMs, which is much more present-oriented than Freud's, focuses on the manifest content of the memory (Adler, 1931, 1937). The theory of infantile amnesia is not relevant to his theory of

EMs. Instead, EMs are seen as revealing fundamental aspects of the individual's present view of life. An individual's EMs are

> the reminders he carries about with him of his own limits and of the meaning of circumstances. . . . [They serve as] a story he repeats to himself to warn him or comfort him, to keep him concentrated on his goal, to prepare him, by means of past experiences, to meet the future with an already tested style of action. (Adler, 1931, p. 72).

Accordingly, an individual selects from his past those events, real or fantasized, which have a bearing on his current situation. Adler (1927) believed that early memories are of particular relevance in depicting one's fundamental attitude toward life. The key factor in the retention of a particular memory was not the unconscious associations to a repressed infantile conflict, but the consistency of the memory with the individual's attitudinal frame of reference, or, in a broader sense, his style of life.

The Adlerian approach to EMs is illustrated by Mosak (1958). A young woman in treatment gave the following two EMs:

> We had a cookie jar on the top shelf in the kitchen. I couldn't reach it by myself, so my uncle lifted me up and I got the cookie jar.
>
> I was sitting on top of a fence. Suddenly, I lost my balance, fell off, and broke my jaw. (p. 305)

Mosak interpreted this set of EMs as reflecting the woman's current view of herself as dependent on others, especially men, for getting her needs met. She felt that, without this support, disaster would ensue. Mosak noted that this woman had married a man who provided her with high social status and material possessions. She came to treatment following a suicide attempt that was precipitated by her husband's having left her.

Adler viewed the EM as a means by which the individual validates and justifies her current view of herself in the world. Therefore, if the style of life changes, parallel changes in the EMs would be expected. Similarly, at the successful completion of therapy, significant EM changes should occur. These changes should be indicated in the emergence of a set of new EMs that reflect a more adaptive style of life or in the modification of maladaptive attitudes apparent in the EMs obtained at the beginning of treatment.

For an historical treatment of the development of Adler's views regarding EMs, the reader is referred to Ansbacher (1973).

DIFFERENCES IN FREUD'S AND ADLER'S VIEWS REGARDING EMs

An important difference between Freud and Adler centers around their views of the principal function of EMs. Freud (1901/1956) described EMs as "concealing"[2] since, in his view, they displace, or cover up, other "really significant impressions" (pp. 33–34). In contrast, Adler (Ansbacher & Ansbacher, 1956) viewed EMs as "revealing" in that they are "reminders . . . [a person] carries about with him of his own limits and of the meaning of circumstances" (p. 351).

These divergent views of how EMs function, in turn, give rise to quite different attitudes and interpretive methods on the part of Freud and Adler toward EMs. Freud (1916/1971) was interested in the phenomenon of childhood amnesia, by which he meant "that the first years of life, up to the age of five, six, or eight, have not left the same traces in memory as our later experiences" (p. 210). He believed that childhood amnesia is a result of the repression of infantile sexual impulses, and he stated that it is "a regular task in psycho-analytic treatment to fill in the blank in infantile memories" (p. 211). Thus, Freud was concerned with forgotten events, memories not accessible to consciousness. Moreover, Freud's goal as an analyst was to bring to awareness the repressed infantile memories, rather than to focus upon the meaning and importance of the early events reported, which was the approach taken by Adler. To sharpen the matter further, it was as if Freud and Adler were addressing two different questions. Freud sought to explain how we remember so little of our very early experience. Adler, on the other hand, seemed most interested in the fact that people selectively retain certain events from a wealth of very early experiences. True, Freud (1916/1971) recognized that "the child no less than the adult only retains in memory what is important" (p. 211), but, as Ansbacher (1947) indicated, Freud seemed more interested in forgetting than in remembering in his writings. In sum, one reason for their difference in viewpoints regarding EMs is that Freud sought to explain the "forgetting" of infantile experience while Adler focused upon the selective retention of certain early experiences.

The lack of systematic investigation of EMs by analytically inclined researchers can be attributed to a central axiom in the Freudian theory of EMs—namely, EMs owe their existence to a process of displacement. Accordingly, what is remembered is of less importance than what is displaced and repressed. For Freudians, the content of EMs is considered important only because of the associative relationship between the EM content and the repressed content that has been displaced. While Freud attached importance to EMs, he attached no more importance to them than he would to any other manifestation of repressed material (e.g., slips of the tongue). Thus, systematic EM research has not been undertaken by researchers with a Freudian orientation.

In contrast to Freud's emphasis upon the process of displacement and repression, Mosak (1958) observed that Adler differed from Freud on the matter of why EMs were retained: "Early memories were retained because of a selective factor in memory, and . . . this selective factor was not repression but rather consistency with the individual's attitudinal frame of reference, the life style" (p. 302). In addition, Adler's view of EMs (Ansbacher & Ansbacher, 1956), raised EMs to a position of special importance:

> [From] the incalculable number of impressions which meet an individual, he chooses to remember only those which he feels, however darkly, to have a bearing on his situation. Thus his memories represent his "Story of My Life"; a story he repeats to himself to warn him or comfort him, to keep him concentrated on his goal, and to prepare him by means of past experiences, so that he will meet the future with an already tested style of action. (p. 351)

Referring to Adler's position, Mosak (1958) observed that the "recollections merely reflected the person's perceptual framework, within which he interpreted life's experiences" (p. 302). Adler's emphasis upon what is "obvious" in the EMs—the organized perceptual framework, self-reminders, and messages that have present relevance—stands in contrast to Freud's view that EMs function to conceal what is significant.

A final area of disagreement concerns causality. In discussing Adler's position, Mosak (1958) stressed that the events referenced in EMs should *not* be regarded as causal. That is, one should not construe the events depicted in EMs as critical formative incidents which have a profound, and perhaps irreversible, impact upon the individual's future development. Similarly, Ansbacher (1973), quoting from Adler's *The Neurotic Constitution* (1912), observed that from the neurotic's perspective the memory image may appear to be of a "traumatic" (after Freud) nature. However, Adler maintained that

> none of these memory images, childhood fantasies, ever functioned pathogenically like a psychic trauma. Only at the outset of the neurosis . . . are the appropriate memory images brought out from material of the distant past. They become significant on account of their usefulness in making neurotic behavior possible and in interpreting it, that is on account of their pertinent relationship. (Ansbacher, 1973, p. 137)

Instead of viewing EMs as traumatic experiences, the Adlerian perceives EMs as containing information that bears strictly upon the indi-

vidual's current perceptual framework. The Freudian position, as articulated by Devereux (1966), provides an interesting contrast. Devereux
argues that it is not the event itself that is traumatic (so far, Adler would
agree), but rather the individual's perception of it at the time the event
occurred:

> The crucial fact here is that *all traumatic memories pertain to an in-
> accurately perceived and experienced situation.* Had the situation been
> perceived and experienced correctly, it would not be *still* traumatic,
> since it would have been mastered in the course of experiencing
> it. (p. 320)

In contrast to Adler, Freud (1905/1938) stressed the determining role
of early childhood experience on current personality functioning.
Freud's views as reproduced below appear in the context of a discussion
of repressive factors related to "infantile sexuality":

> I refer to the peculiar amnesia which veils from most people (not
> from all) the first years of their childhood, usually the first six or
> eight years. So far, it has not occurred to us that this amnesia should
> surprise us, though we have good reasons for it. For we are in-
> formed that during those years which have left nothing except for
> a few incomprehensible memory fragments, we have vividly reacted
> to impressions, that we have expressed love, jealousy and other
> passions as they then affected us.... On the other hand we must
> assume, or we may convince ourselves through psychological ob-
> servations of others, that the very impressions which we have for-
> gotten have nevertheless left the deepest traces in psychic life, and
> *acted as determinants for our whole future development.* We conclude
> therefore that we do not deal with a real forgetting of infantile
> impressions but rather with an amnesia similar to that observed in
> neurotics for later experiences, the nature of which consists in their
> being kept away from consciousness (repression). (pp. 581–582;
> emphasis mine)

Freud viewed early experience, remembered or not, as having determined the whole course of personality development. Adlerians, on the
other hand, represent early recollections as larger than life "myths"
which owe their preservation to present attitudes. Adlerians believe that
the individual's current attitudes "sound out" and bring into awareness
those EMs which encapsulate early learnings having current relevance.

SIMILARITIES IN FREUD'S AND ADLER'S VIEWS REGARDING EMs

The differences between Freud and Adler regarding the importance of early childhood recollections have been sharpened by Adlerians. The similarity in their views can be seen in Freud's account (1910/1957) of "Leonardo da Vinci and a Memory of His Childhood" when he draws an analogy between the nature of EMs and the manner in which the writing of history originated among the peoples of antiquity:

> [The] nature [of EMs] is perhaps best illustrated by a comparison with the way in which the writing of history originated among the peoples of antiquity. As long as a nation was small and weak it gave no thought to the writing of its history. Men tilled the soil of their land, fought for their existence against their neighbours, and tried to gain territory from them and to acquire wealth. It was an age of heroes, not of historians. (p. 83)

The dynamics of the situation described above by Freud approximates the meaning of the Adlerian term "striving for superiority." Continuing the analogy, Freud then describes an "age of reflection" during which men felt themselves to be rich and powerful and began to feel a need to learn where they had come from and how they had developed. Accordingly, historical writing began to look into the past,

> gathered traditions and legends, interpreted the traces of antiquity that survived in customs and usages, and in this way created a history of the past. It was inevitable that this early history should have been an expression of *present beliefs and wishes* rather than a true picture of the past; for many things had been dropped from the nation's memory, while others were distorted, and *some remains of the past were given a wrong interpretation in order to fit in with contemporary ideas.* (p. 83; emphasis mine)

In the above analogy Freud strongly implies that EMs reflect present beliefs and attitudes, which is exactly the position of Adler. In sum, while Freud emphasized that EMs were screens that concealed more significant clinical material, he also appeared to recognize the relevance of EMs to current beliefs and attitudes.

Despite the similarity of their views on the importance of EMs, Freud's interpretive approach differs from the Adlerian method, as Rom (1965) illustrated with Goethe's earliest recollections. Rom emphasizes that the interpretive approach of Adlerians is individualizing, or idiographic, whereas Freud's method, within the framework of psychoanalytic theory, is generalizing, or nomothetic.

Mayman (1968/1984a) was also struck by Freud's analogy between EMs and a nation's view of its own history. It is likely that Freudians, Adlerians, most ego psychologists, and Cognitive-Perceptualists would all agree with Mayman when he writes:

> This is a provocative view of the purpose of writing history. We sometimes laugh at countries which rewrite their history books to fit with major political trends. But this only does openly what history books in all countries do tacitly without quite realizing it. A prime purpose of writing history, at least history as taught in grade schools, is to instil in children an ideology, to give them a common set of myths to live by, to choose for them the kinds of heroes with whom to identify and to embody in the legends of their culture the values on which their group identity rests. It is therefore entirely appropriate, or at least understandable, that the American view of the American Revolution, for example, be quite different from the English view. The history of the revolution for Americans is a very selective report of what happened, in order to establish for Americans as a group one of the important landmarks in the development of their group identity. (p. 125, fn)

THE EGO-PSYCHOLOGICAL VIEW OF EMs

An analysis of recent thinking about EMs by ego psychologists suggests that a synthesis of early Freudian and Adlerian notions has taken place. Ego psychologists seek to supplement the early psychoanalytical concentration on the sexual and aggressive content of drives, impulses, and fantasies with increased attention to how the structure of the personality deals with this content (e.g., Hartmann, 1958, 1964). Mayman (1968/1984a), who is representative of this trend in EM analysis, views EMs as an expression

> of important fantasies around which a person's character-structure is organized.... [They] are selected unconsciously by a person to conform with and confirm ingrained images of himself and others. ... The themes which bind together the *dramatis personae* of a person's earliest memories define nuclear relationship patterns which are likely to repeat themselves isomorphically in a wide range of other life situations.... [In analyzing EMs] it is as important ... to know about the ego, its designs, its ways of maintaining repression as it is to know about that which is repressed. (pp. 123–124)

In this passage we see elements of Adler's emphasis on the present in terms of the EM's "confirming" images of self and others as well as the Freudian emphasis on the importance of early nuclear relationships and the operation of repression in EM formation.

In a similar manner, Burnell and Solomon (1964), Chess (1951), and Langs, Rothenberg, Fishman, and Reiser (1960) all take an "ego approach" to the EM in that they view the production as a method of coping with conflicts through fantasy. The ego-psychological approach views the EM as an unconscious attempt by the individual to integrate, synthesize, and resolve conflicts by reactivating childhood experiences of similar emotional content. Influential factors in shaping the EM include past life experiences, present level of personality organization, current life stress, and cultural milieu (Kramer, Ornstein, Whitman, & Baldridge, 1967).

Chess (1951) exemplified this approach in her report of a girl in therapy. Chess traced the production of her client's EMs to her needs at the time of memory formation as well as at the point of recall. Her thirteen-year-old client recalled that, at age seven, she used to have many friends but was kept from playing with them by her overly protective, critical mother. Chess discussed this EM in terms of the girl's need to defend against the reality of being an isolated, rather dependent seven year old as well as in relation to her current struggle to separate from her mother, whom she perceived as hostile.

A major divergence of the ego psychology movement from classical Freudian analysis is evident in the belief that much can be learned from the manifest content of the EM without the necessity of intensive free association to the particular aspects of the memory (e.g., Langs et al., 1960; Langs & Reiser, 1961; Levy, 1965; Levy & Grigg, 1962; Saul, Snyder, & Sheppard, 1956). The manifest content is viewed not just as a screen to distort the latent meaning of the EM, but also as a reflection of the individual's ability to manage the latent content. Mayman (1968/1984a) argued that this adaptive function is just as important as the content of the repressed material.

Mayman's Ego-Psychological Approach

As an ego psychologist, Mayman (1968/1984a, 1963/1984b) has contributed several major papers that provide a conceptual bridge between an id-psychological view of EMs and Adler's position. His paper (1968/1984a) as President of the Society for Personality Assessment, a classic, is perhaps the most complete articulation of ego-psychological theory and application.

Once we conceptualize EMs as projective data, it is more accurate to regard EMs as fantasies than as facts. Mayman's position (1968/1984a), consistent with Kris' (1956a, 1956b), is to regard them as "personal myths":

> If we are moved . . . to take the most extreme position regarding early memories, we would come to view all early memories not as autobiographical, factual reports, but rather as "personal myths", . . . that is, as inventions which may have little or no relevance to actual events but great relevance to the personal themes which affect the way a person experiences events. Given this assumption, we are free to analyze early memories as projected fantasies, much as we now analyze TAT themes. (p. 128)

If the proposition that EMs are "personal myths" is accepted, one can readily make the transition from an id-psychology—with its distrust of manifest content—to an ego-psychology, which is interested in the products of ego functioning. Mayman (1968/1984a) describes that transition:

> with the advent of psychoanalytic ego psychology . . . the screen function of consciousness came to take on a double meaning. Perceptions, fantasies, [and] random thoughts which served the ego's countercathetic purposes, were seen to carry traces of the unconscious contents they were intended to mask. Like any good disguise, surface appearance represents a skillful blend of the camouflaging design and the images one wishes to hide.
>
> In the fifty years which have elapsed from the time when psychoanalysis was largely an id-psychology, we have come to see that the distrust of manifest content is appropriate only in the context of an id-psychology. Today it is as important to the psychoanalyst to know about the ego, its designs, its ways of maintaining repression, as it is to know about that which is repressed. And, just as the latent content of conscious thought processes reveals much about the vicissitudes of the id, the manifest contents of these experiences reveal much about the workings of the ego. (pp. 122–123)

It is not possible to do justice to Mayman's skill at interpreting EMs in this brief discussion, so the reader is urged to refer to his papers. However, Mayman's (1968/1984a) interpretation of the following set of EMs obtained from a female adolescent in-patient will serve to illustrate his technique:

> I had a little white kitten that I had found and was taking care of. Mother wouldn't let me keep the cat in at night. I remember this very cold night, it was snowy and icy outside. I begged her to let the cat stay in but she didn't even listen to me. The next morning

when I woke up and looked out the window, the cat's guts and blood were all over the street. It had been run over during the night.

Another time I came home sick from school. I had such an awful pain in my stomach, I was doubled over and couldn't stand up. It hurt me so badly I thought I was going to die. She just laughed at me and kept telling me it served me right for eating all that candy when she told me not to. (pp. 128–129)

Mayman's (1968/1984a) comments and interpretations follow below.

There were no representations of a good mother in her set of twelve early memories. In fact, all of the really early memories of mother had been wholly blotted out; both of these memories were placed at 7 or 8 years of age. This girl's almost nightmarish inversion of the more normal image of mother; her feeling that she was at the mercy of a woman who was less like a mother than she was like a fairy-tale version of the evil witch or the cruel step-mother; and, by implication, the girl's enduring sense of impotent rage at this mother who makes such a mockery of the nurturant care the girl so much craved, all imply severe pathology in the expectancies she carried with her into any and all potentially nurturant relationships. These and her other early memories are representative samples of an inner world in which she experiences object-ties as empty, predatory and cold-blooded.

The presenting symptom in this case was murder. The girl had killed her mother by feeding her poison, and watched her die writhing in pain, laughing at her mother all the while, just as the mother allegedly laughed at her in her earliest memory. The kitten memory was reported after sentence had been passed, during the initial intake interviews at the state hospital where she had been confined. The stomach-ache memory was not recalled until two and a half years later, after two years of psychotherapy. (p. 129)

Of all ego psychologists, Mayman is the most articulate and specific in proposing a system for the interpretation of EMs. Mayman adopts a thematic approach that follows classic psychoanalytic stages of development. Mayman's (1968/1984a) introduction to his interpretive system is presented below verbatim, as is his interpretive system.

The themes around which people build their retrospectively convincing views of life as they lived it, run the gamut from . . . archaic themes to some quite mature forms of object relation. A distribution of themes implicit in early memories, collected more or less randomly from normal, neurotic, borderline and psychotic subjects, is summarized in Table [2.1], and illustrates the variety of "oral," "anal," "phallic," and "genital" self-representations and object-representations which commonly appear in early memories. The psychosexual terms are meant to designate developmental phases from which the relationship paradigm is drawn, rather than to refer to the more narrowly instinctual meanings of these terms as used in a psychoanalytic id-psychology. As used here these terms define a multiplicity of different ego-states, each organized around a distinctive affect and self-experience, and made up of a definitive need, a need-appropriate object-relationship and self-representation, and phase-appropriate conflicts, defenses and compromise formations, and ego-competencies. Implicit in an ego-state may be oral, anal, or phallic impulses but these impulses become accessible to the ego (and to the therapist of a patient) not in id-terms as raw impulses, but by way of ego derivatives including, most importantly, such ego-states [Mayman, 1963/1984b]. Implicit in all the "oral" themes listed in Table [2.1] may be a primal hunger for nurturant supplies, an oral hunger which was once experienced by the person in its most archaically literal sense, but the primal oral wish appears in the memory only in its derivative form, as the product of an ego which itself carries the imprint of prior life experiences. Early memories organized around the oral-paradigm depict what the informant's ego and superego have made of the primal wish, rather than that wish itself. Whether the themes express oral optimism and the sense of basic trust, or oral misanthropy and mistrust, they refer to derivative states, adaptive or defensive positions taken by the person toward the still salient, still unfulfilled oral need. (pp. 130–131)

Mayman identifies the most meaningful clinical aspects of EMs from an ego-psychological viewpoint as relationship paradigms, coping style, self-structure, imagoes, and defense modes. These aspects are organized around a series of questions reproduced in Table 2.2.

Mayman's writings on early memories represent a high-water mark from an ego-psychological perspective. His presidential address (1968/1984a) to the Society for Personality Assessment should be read by anyone who wishes to employ this model to interpret EMs.

SUMMARY AND CONCLUSIONS

Three theoretical approaches to EMs have been delineated: Freud's, Adler's, and a composite ego-psychological model. Each stands on its

Table 2.1
Prototypical Interpersonal Themes in Early Memories

I. "Oral" Configurations

    1. Themes of basic mistrust:

        a. Danger of personal extinction by abandonment, starvation, suffocation, being swallowed; sense of engulfing evil and impending doom. (Reminiscent of M. Klein's "paranoid position.")

Oral
Pessimism

        b. Bleak, empty aloneness; anaclitic depression; themes of getting lost, being sent away from home more or less permanently, death of parents; themes of traumatic separation and of depression verging on despair. (Reminiscent of Melanie Klein's "depressive position.")

    2. Deprivation or insufficient supplies of attention, food or love: oral pessimism, dissatisfaction, bitter resentment, sense of unfulfillment (rather than of despair as in I.1).

        a. Temporary separation from others: parents are off by themselves and not aware of the child; child is sent off to school or to other relatives; feeling left out of some adult activities; all of which give rise to a poignant sense of not belonging.

        b. Other themes of deprivation: insufficient supplies of comfort, reassurance, love, attention, care or food; dissatisfied with one's lot.

        c. Loss of some treasured object.

        d. Suffering an unpleasant or dangerous illness.

    3. Aggressive reactions to deprivation or frustration: demanding or grasping needed supplies rather than merely yearning for them as in I.2.

        a. Suffused with impotent rage.

        b. Greedy hunger for what one does not have: taking and holding onto, appropriating by snatching away, grasping, or biting.

        c. Resentment—and/or malicious treatment of—younger sibling.

        d. Meets with punishment, criticism or "accidental" injury as a direct consequence of oral-aggressive behavior.

    4. Gratification themes: sense of snugness, security, basic trust, expectation of fulfillment; sense of personal worth; availability of external comforts and supports.

Oral
Optimism

        a. Snug pleasures of sleep, bed, breast, bath, food, or physical closeness.

        b. Comforting care during an illness.

        c. Close comforting attentive presence of mother or mother surrogate. (Father may fill this role at times.)

        d. Receiving gifts as proof of love with ensuing sense of warmth, belonging, and fulfillment.

        e. Being helped by an adult to learn to look after oneself, e.g., being taught one's name and address, how to tie one's shoes.

    5. Gratification themes with a reversal of roles so that one becomes the giver rather than the recipient of nurturant care.

        a. Taking the nurturing parent role toward a younger sib, pet, friend or sick parent.

Table 2.1 (continued)

II. "Anal" Configuations: Self-Differentiating Relationship Paradigms

    1. Retentiveness: willful stubbornness, defiance, passive-aggressive noncompliance.

Passive
Aggressive
        a. Withholding from adults; sulking.

        b. Defiance by refusal to comply with adult's requests—including food fads, refusal to eat, refusal to go to bed.

        c. Passive aggressive "inability" to produce what is asked for or expected by adults.

    [p.] add [p.] if: Meets with punishment, ridicule, or attack upon one's self-esteem by a superego-figure due to one's retentive behavior.

    2. Expulsiveness: hurting self or others by dirtying them or treating them like dirt.

Hurting
Self
        a. Insufficient sphincter control (usually with memory of shame, guilt or punishment); other forms of being dirtied or feeling oneself to be unclean.

        b. Being the object of vilification; being treated by other "like shit."

Hurting
Others
        c. Defiance by vilification, spitting, demeaning others, throwing things (especially rocks, dirt or mud); treating others "like dirt" or extruding others by pushing them away or keeping them at a distance.

    add [p.] if: Meets with punishment, ridicule, or injury to one's self-esteem due to one's extrusive-aggressive behavior.

    3. Sublimation or reaction formations:

        a. Doing what one is supposed to do, avoiding conflicts with coercive parents.

        b. Attention to cleanliness, cleaning up, being clean.

        c. Preoccupation with one's own or another's possessions, with emphasis on quantity, orderliness and ownership.

III. "Phallic-Intrusive" and "Phallic-Locomotor" Configurations: Pleasure in Mastery; Pleasure in Proofs of One's Prowess, Strength or Competence

    1. Active forms:

        a. Expressing initiative, independence or eager curiosity; going off on one's own, wandering away to explore one's surroundings.

        b. Boisterous play usually with peers; vigorous activity including physical attack; mischievously teasing play.

        c. Active use of "phallic-locomotor" conveyance, with emphasis on the vehicles which carry one to adventures and new places; riding a bicycle, riding a horse, going on a trip. (Being taken for a drive should be listed as III.2b)

        d. Competitive games: enjoyment of competition, pleasure in conquest, insistence on asserting one's dominance over people or impersonal obstacles (to be distinguished from the "greedy hunger" of I.3b). Proving one is not inferior—being as good as someone else.

        e. Identification with father; admiring father and wanting to be like him, to use his tools like him, to fix things as he does.

        f. Setting fires and enjoying the ensuing excitement.

    add [p.] if: Any of these activities culminate in physical injury, narcissistic insult, or physical punishment.

---

[1] A "p." (punishment) "score" is added to a previous score when an activity meets with some form of injury, narcissistic hurt, or punishment.

Table 2.1 (continued)

    2. Passive forms:

      a. Passively watching large moving vehicles or other wondrous objects; watching fires (but not setting them); watching the feats of others.

      b. Being taken for a ride by an adult.

      c. Being teased, being tossed about playfully by an adult, or carried by father in horse-and-rider play.

      d. Admiration and envy of phallic objects of others (symbolic or real); disappointment and unfavorable comparison with one's own phallic object or prowess; yearning to do as well as one's ego-models.

[1]add [p.] if: Any of these activities culminate in injury, narcissistic insult, or punishment.

    3. Being the object of phallic-aggressive assault.

      a. Being knocked down and overpowered by brute strength; fantasy of being whipped or beaten.

      b. Fear of dangerous, brutish creatures (including ghosts and bogeymen).

      c. Being shy, timid, fearful of exercising initiative.

      d. Themes of physical injury: actual injury to the genitals, symbolic castration themes.

      e. Being hurt physically by a doctor; tonsil or other operation on body members.

IV. "Phallic-sexual" Configurations: Activities which are Frankly Sexual or Veiled but Recognizably Sexual in Nature

    1. Intrusive forms: moving outward to make contact with sexual object.

      a. Playful, sexually tinged curiosity or exhibitionism; sex play or secretive, sexually tinged play with peers; interested examination of the sex organs of others but only as a "passive bystander."

      b. Proud or excited self-display, usually sublimated in dancing, singing or performing in some other manner before an audience of potential admirers. The accent here is on *doing* something to win favor, not *standing* by, *waiting* or *expecting* to be admired as in IV.2b.

      c. Shame or embarrassment rather than pleasure following intrusive self-display.

[1]add [p.] if: Intrusive sexual activity leads to physical injury, narcissistic insult, or physical punishment.

    2. Inceptive forms: trying to excite a sexually desired object to make a frank or veiled sexual approach.

      a. Being fetchingly coy, seductive; trying to make oneself attractive and endearing; teasing others in a sexually provocative manner.

      b. Pleasure in one's appearance; attention to pretty clothes, attractive grooming; pleasure in being looked at, noticed, admired or photographed.

      c. Shame or embarrassment rather than pleasure following inceptive self-display.

[1]add [p.] if: Inceptive sexual activity leads to physical injury, narcissistic insult, or physical punishment.

---

[1]A "p." (punishment) "score" is added to a previous score when an activity meets with some form of injury, narcissistic hurt, or punishment.

Table 2.1 (continued)

V. "Oedipal" Configurations: Competitive Striving to Win Favor With a Love-Object

   1. Male relationship patterns:

Hostile
Competitive

     a. Jealousy or rivalry (with father or a sibling) for the affection of mother or a mother surrogate; interest in mother's doings with another male.

     b. Failure to win mother's love, often accompanied by self-blame for one's personal inadequacy.

     c. Resentment or fear of the father as an overt or tacit rival for mother's love.

     d. Conflict between parents in which the child sides with the mother and rejects the father; angry at father for hurting mother.

Positive
Harmonious

     e. Denial of Oedipal conflict by stress on the warm, harmonious relationships with both mother and father.

     f. Doing things with mother which are pleasureful and exciting, with the father tacitly excluded.

     g. Pleasure in bringing mother a phallic gift.

   2. Female relationship patterns:

Hostile
Competitive

     a. Jealousy or rivalry with mother or a sibling for the affection of father or a father surrogate; interest in father's doings with another female.

     b. Resentment or fear of mother as an avowed or tacit rival for father's love.

     c. Failure to win father's love, with accompanying sense of personal inadequacy.

     d. Conflict between parents in which the child sides with father and rejects the mother.

Positive
Harmonious

     e. Denial of Oedipal conflict by stressing the warm, harmonious, noncompetitive aspects of one's relationship with mother in the family triangle.

     f. Doing exciting or pleasureful things with father, with mother tacitly excluded.

     g. Interest in having a baby as mother did; or receiving some symbolically equivalent phallic gift from father; interest in pregnancy and childbirth.

     h. Playing house, playing with dolls, dressing up in mother's clothes, or in some other way doing as mother does.

VI. "Latency" Configurations: More Sublimated Peer-Group Activities

   1. Productivity and positive self-esteem.

     a. Socialization with peers; group play with well-differentiated roles.

     b. Industriousness, learning to do things, constructing and planning with others in a common endeavor.

     c. Turning manipulative skills to creative accomplishment.

   2. Inferiority:

     a. Withdrawal from, isolation in, or rejection by one's peer group.

SOURCE: Mayman, 1968/1984a.

NOTE: Mayman notes that early memories can be "scored" using the notational schema employed in this table.

Table 2.2

Clinically Meaningful Aspects of the Analysis of a Set of Early Recollections

Relationship Paradigms

1. To what extent does one represent himself as living in lonely isolation? In close interaction with others? How wide a range of relationships comes spontaneously to mind? To what extent do mother, father, other family members, and friends "people" the patient's intrapsychic world?

2. What forms of relatedness seem most congenial, most ego-syntonic, easiest to maintain?

3. What is the quality and intensity of feeling implicit in these relationships? What is the "level" of relationship--impersonal? anaclitic? imitative? mutual?

4. Is there evidence of particular psychosexual paradigms serving as models for interpersonal relationships? Evidence of preferred psychosexual positions to escape from other more dangerous positions?

Coping Style

5. Does the patient represent himself as active or as passive in his relationships? If active, how? compliant? courageous? venturesome? defiant? autonomous? assertive? self-sufficient? If passive, what form of passivity? timid? self-abasing? compliant? limp? "feeling" and "watching," rather than "doing?"

Self-structure

6. Where is a person's "self-feeling" most fully invested? In which modalities of experience? sensual? kinaesthetic? affective? introspective? extroceptive? What forms of activity does the person readily invest himself in, and in which can he not invest himself?

7. What kinds of life-experiences seem ego-syntonic and which, by exclusion, ego-alien? Which qualities of experience remain split off from the self? Which threaten to disorganize the sense of self (i.e., are not only estranged but bring on some depersonalization)?

Imagoes

8. What are the principal representations of mother, father, and self? What is the principal representation of the self in relation to others? In what roles are the significant-others cast?

9. Are there traces of multiple or conflicting representations of significant-others and of oneself?

10. Which self-representations seem to have been encouraged or fostered by the parents? Which seem to have been incorporated into the ego-ideal?

Defense Modes

11. To what extent do "primal" or archaic memories occur?

12. To what extent is there a masochistic fixation upon fears, disappointments, dangers, injuries, pain, or illness?

13. How much repression do we encounter? To what extent does the patient feel himself cut off from his infantile origins, i.e., early sources of pleasure and early object-ties? How vague or nebulous are the memories? How selective is the memory process?

14. What defenses other than repression appear in the way in which the story is told? isolation? reaction-formation? projection? denial?

15. To what extent are memories phobic? depressive? self-punitive? counter-phobic? withdrawn? conflict-avoidant? shallow? self-preoccupied? warm and human?

own merits and has its particular implications for diagnosis, assessment, and treatment.

The classical Freudian approach requires considerable inference and uncovering on the part of the clinician since what is "manifest" is thought to cover significant, latent, repressed events. Nonetheless, Robert Langs and his group (1960, 1961, 1965a, 1965b, 1967) developed a procedure that they have successfully used in EM research.

Adlerians have used EMs diagnostically to formulate a style of life for the client. As they view it, a style of life is less than adequate to the extent that the individual has not developed "social interest." However, whether the life style results in problems in living depends upon whether the interpersonal environment supports or frustrates the individual's accustomed life style. Adlerians have also used EMs to gauge the effectiveness of psychotherapy outcome (e.g., Eckstein, 1976).

The ego-psychological approach to EMs has incorporated parts of both Freudian and Adlerian views of EMs. This method straddles the past and the present, viewing the past in terms of the individual's current functioning. Emphasis is placed on determining how the defenses function, as well as on uncovering that which has been repressed. Mayman's system (1968/1984a) for analyzing EMs is the model that is currently followed in the area.

With the historical review of EM theory complete, the Cognitive-Perceptual model is presented in Chapter 3, a theory of personality that is based on individual differences in the organization of memory.

NOTES

1. This chapter is a revised version of a paper originally published in the *Journal of Personality Assessment* in 1982, entitled, "Earliest Childhood Memories: Four Theoretical Perspectives," by the writer and Jeffrey Last. Permission from the *Journal of Personality Assessment* to reproduce parts of this paper is gratefully acknowledged.

2. It should be noted that there are substantial differences in word choice among Freud's translators. What Brill renders as "concealed memories" (S. Freud 1901/1956, p. 33), for example, is translated "screen memories" in *The Standard Edition of the Complete Works of Sigmund Freud* (S. Freud 1901/1960, p. 43).

3

THE COGNITIVE-
PERCEPTUAL MODEL AND
EARLY MEMORIES

The past is being continually remade, reconstructed in the interests
of the present. . . .

F. C. Bartlett

It is difficult, and probably impossible, to conceptualize a model of personality that does not presuppose the existence of an adequately functioning autobiographical memory. Without an intact autobiographical
memory, we would have no way of knowing who we are, who others
are, what the world is like, or what to expect from life. Developing and
maintaining a fundamental set of beliefs to regulate our lives would be
impossible. Drives might exist intact, but the individual would lack the
inner resources and experiential base to satisfy them. Perhaps the closest
analog to an individual who cannot access his autobiographical memory
is a patient with advanced Alzheimer's disease. It can therefore be posited
that autobiographical memory is absolutely basic and essential to any
conceptualization of personality grounded in self psychology.

Although easily intuited, autobiographical memory is not easily defined. Autobiographical memory can be regarded functionally as that
aspect of memory which provides an identity to the self, especially the
self in relation to others and to the world. A similar problem with definition applies to memory. Neisser (1982) observed that it makes more
sense to consider the function of memory rather than attempt a strict
scientific definition:

Although I am far from sure how to classify the phenomena of
memory, I must put them in some kind of order to discuss them

at all. Science cannot proceed without some way of defining things so we can set out to study them. The organization I will use is based on the functions of memory. What do we use the past *for*?" (p. 13)

Earlier, in discussing memory, Neisser (1982) notes:

> I think that "memory" in general does not exist. . . . It is a concept left over from a medieval psychology that partitioned the mind into independent faculties: "thought" and "will" and "emotion" and many others, with "memory" among them. Let's give it up, and begin to ask our questions in different ways. (p. 12)

The remarks that Neisser made about the function of memory apply to autobiographical memory as well. It therefore makes sense to take a functional approach to defining autobiographical memory.

Arguably the best current test of autobiographical memory extant is early childhood memories (EMs). Many professionals are confused, however, as to how EMs should be used. Although many insight-oriented clinicians report that they use EMs in treatment, most are not clear about how they use EMs or even whether they view EMs as real events, traumas, historical fictions, screens, metaphors, or as fantasies about the past.

The Cognitive-Perceptual (CP) model (Bruhn, 1984, 1985, 1990; Bruhn & Bellow, 1984, 1987; Bruhn & Last, 1982) treats EMs as fantasies about the past that reveal present concerns. While it is acknowledged that many EMs are firmly rooted in a substrate of reality, the CP model maintains that interpretations can be made without having to validate the EM for accuracy. In other words, the interpretation will be valid even if the memory has been distorted by unconscious forces or fabricated entirely.

The CP model has been formulated to help us understand how we perceive ourselves, others and the world around us. In this sense, CP theory is a theory of personality that is grounded on memory process rather than drives (psychoanalysis), fictive final goals (Adlerian theory), or reinforcement (social learning theory). To understand the process of perception, we must understand how data is organized in autobiographical memory. CP theory posits that autobiographical memory employs a relatively stable set of schema for perceptual data being scanned. Schemas are created consistent with the principle of utility—we attend to and remember what has the greatest perceived usefulness or that which makes us most adaptive. Information that does not fit existing schemas is unlikely to be processed and stored.

Cognitive-Perceptual theory differs in several crucial respects from social learning theory, with which it is sometimes compared. The latter, which focuses on how we learn, explains human behavior via reinforcers and related concepts. By contrast, CP theory considers all that we have learned—whether by reinforcement, conditioning, modeling, or osmosis—and examines the material that has survived the longest (EMs) for clues as to how the individual perceives himself and his world. What powers CP theory—the analog to drive reduction in psychoanalysis—is the individual's desire, however conflicted, to increase the range and scope of his or her adaptability or personal competence.

Because we are primarily concerned in these books with EMs and their clinical application, we will begin by assuming in our theoretical discussion of the CP model that our average person has considerable experience with the world and has accordingly formed a relatively stable set of schemas in autobiographical memory. The CP model does not require this assumption, however, and could easily begin by incorporating and expanding upon Piaget's work with cognitive development in newborn and young children.

CP theory is intended to function as a scientific model that can generate accurate predictions regarding individual behavior. CP theory should, in time, prove to be a formidable predictive model, because individuals tend to behave consistent with their perceptions, attitudes, and expectations. Empirical results with criminal populations (Bruhn & Davidow, 1983; Davidow & Bruhn, 1990) support this premise.

AUTOBIOGRAPHICAL MEMORY AND ITS ORGANIZATION

The organization of autobiographical memory is a complex matter. *Attitude* and *mood* appear to be the major determinants of whether a memory can be accessed at all. That is, if one's present mood is inconsistent with the mood of a particular memory, that memory may be difficult or impossible to retrieve so long as the discrepancy in mood remains. The same principle holds for attitude. It is not accurate to say that such memories are "forgotten;" it is closer to the truth to say that they cannot be accessed so long as present attitudes and mood interfere with, or block, their remembrance.

CP theory postulates that autobiographical memory conforms to the principles of adaptation and utility. That is, important memories are given priority in autobiographical memory. There are several reasons why a memory might be important. A memory may preserve a major lesson learned about the self, others, or the world, or it may focus on major issues that are unresolved and currently in process.

It is one thing to argue that autobiographical memory conforms to principles of utility and adaptation; it is another to specify *precisely* how autobiographical memory is organized. To address this matter in depth is beyond the scope of this chapter, but seven specific organizing principles can be described at this time: (1) attitude; (2) mood or state; (3) category; (4) time; (5) person; (6) place; and (7) activity. Of these, the two most important appear to be attitude and mood.

The principle of attraction regulates the emergence of recollections from long-term memory. As we believe, so we remember. *Attitude* is the single most powerful organizing influence in autobiographical memory. Once a powerful, highly generalized attitude is embraced ("People are not to be trusted" or "If I am willing to work hard, I can achieve my goals") the individual's universe of autobiographical memories is reorganized to give expression to this attitude. For instance, if an individual is deeply hurt by someone and comes to believe that people in general are not trustworthy, he may come to "forget" how his first-grade teacher was kind to him and sensitive to his feelings. Why? Because this recollection is inconsistent with a major attitude that regulates his current recall of past experiences. He may suddenly remember that his first-grade teacher, whom he previously recalled liking very much, hurt his feelings once because she would not let him go to the bathroom when he asked. Highly generalized attitudes thus function as *gatekeepers* in autobiographical memory and screen out recollections containing attitudes that are inconsistent. As Bartlett (1932) pointed out, memories are ordinarily reconstructions that are organized around general attitudes. Memories as a general rule are more *attitude-sensitive* than *fact-sensitive*. As a result, facts tend to be bent, distorted, or "forgotten" to mesh with a major attitude, as opposed to attitudes being adjusted to conform to the facts. In the realm of memory, attitudes, not facts, dominate. The old line, "Don't bother me with the facts," was never more valid than in the case of autobiographical memory and its organization.

But what happens when a major attitude changes? Assume, for example, that the individual who formerly believed that individuals are not to be trusted abandons this attitude. Will his memories remain as they were, or will they change to reflect his new attitude?

Once the premise is accepted that memory is organized adaptively, the answer can be deduced—the individual's memories must change. His prior set of readily accessible memories has been invalidated and rendered obsolete by the change in his belief structure. The only reason that he would have to retain these antiquated memories is to remind himself of how he used to think, which is not a parsimonious use of high priority memory storage. Ultimately, however, whether autobiographical memories change with a change in attitudes is an empirical question. My experience as a psychotherapist has indicated that, when a client's attitudes change, memories change concurrently. Moreover, it is difficult for most clients to remember their old beliefs and attitudes. For instance, in a conceptually fascinating experiment, Bach (1952) recorded specific memories from clients in the course of their treatment. At the end of treatment, when he asked them to sort out which memories were theirs and which were not, Bach found that his clients tended to deny and disavow their own memories at the end of treatment when these memories no longer meshed with their present attitudes.

The second most important organizing principle with respect to autobiographical memory is *mood*. There are a variety of ways that this point can be demonstrated. Consider, for example, groups of individuals who are characterized by extreme affective liability, for instance, manic depressives. One would predict that if EMs are influenced to any significant extent by mood, manic depressives would show considerable variability in their EMs when their mood changed. That is exactly what appears to happen. Either a new selection of EMs, which mirrors present mood, is pulled from long-term memory or existing EMs are reworked so that the affective component of the memory reflects current mood. Several empirical studies (see the discussion of reliability in Volume II) strongly support the hypothesis that present mood exerts a major influence on what is recalled from long-term memory and how these memories are recalled. I experienced a personal demonstration of this hypothesis when my cat died suddenly and unexpectedly of a heart attack. Having no *spontaneous* memories of losses or deaths, I was amazed to experience a flood of memories of losses when I realized that my cat was dead. These seldom-recalled memories burst into awareness when the grief associated with my loss registered. Two days later, when my acute feelings of grief passed, I could not remember what I had so vividly recalled only a short time before. Many high-affect memories are *state dependent* in that they can be recalled more easily and much more vividly when presently experienced affect mirrors the affect imbued in the memory. Similarly, anxious individuals will tend to recall EMs in which anxiety is the key affective component; the same holds for depression, anger, and other prominent negative affects.

The third organizing principle is *content category*. Although spontaneous EMs play out unresolved issues that are currently being processed, autobiographical memory contains many more memories that can be brought into awareness when the proper categorical probe is used. For instance, an individual's spontaneous EMs may deal only with the achievements of various sorts. Achievement is an example of a content category. But the same individual may be able to recall memories that pertain to other content categories if they are probed correctly. For example, if we wanted to probe punishment as a content category, we might ask, "What is your first recollection of being punished? Your clearest recollection? The most severe punishment you ever received? The time that you felt worst after being punished? The most unfair punishment?" Such questions reflect our intuitive understanding that autobiographical memory—at least in our culture—is organized to recognize the significance of punishment as a content category. Memories in some categories may contain useful data, or they may contain data that is not currently important. In either case, data stored in categories that are not spotlighted in spontaneous EMs are usually not the focus of immediate interest. Only in a small minority of cases—e.g., the most traumatic memory—is it clear that the category being probed has major current importance for the individual.

The fourth organizing principle is *time*, which typically involves year and/or age. Time as a category is highly valued in industrialized man, as opposed to native peoples. Native peoples may recall that an event occurred during a season of the year, but they rarely organize events by how old they were at the time or by a particular year in which the event occurred. Industrialized man, with his emphasis on formal schooling, is more likely to recall that something happened when he was eight, or in the first grade, or in 1968. One's year in school is a common way of ordering autobiographical memory in childhood, adolescence, and young adulthood. In adulthood, autobiographical memory tends to be organized around important life events—the birth of a child, a move, the death of a parent, a job change, a new manager, and so on.

The fifth principle is *person*. Information in this category has considerable adaptive value as it provides data from which the individual first constructs a schema for self, mother, father, sister, brother, teacher, and so on. These individual schemas later generalize into broader schemas, such as "men," "women," and "authority figures." This organizing principle permits the individual to gain ready access to data that has enormous adaptive value: what he can expect from others as individuals, as categories of individuals (athletes, police), and collectively (people generally).

The sixth principle is *place*. Examples of common place categories include school, grandma's house, and church. Place categories help us to organize memories that contain important *expectations* associated with places or situations involving places. For example, the probe, "seated at the kitchen table for dinner," may elicit a series of significant memories that play out expectations of what is likely to occur when the family comes together. Similarly, "taking a test at school" is likely to elicit attitudes about the self in one type of achievement situation and to reveal generalized expectations that the individual has in test-taking situations.

The seventh principle is *activity*. Such activities as swimming, playing kickball, or sex are likely to elicit a number of potentially important memories. Playing kickball, for instance, may access attitudes and feelings related to mastery, self-concept, self-confidence, and peer relationships. Sex is likely to tap material related to self-concept, self-esteem, self-confidence, and cooperation.

Most important memories are redundantly stored in several categories. Assume, for instance, that an individual recalls a spontaneous EM of being punished by his father for something he should not have done. Such a memory may be stored under such categories as punishment (a content category), guilt feelings (mood or state), and father (person). When the same memory is accessed by several directed memory probes (e.g., first memory of being punished, first memory of father, first family memory, etc.), there is strong reason to believe that the memory is important. *Any memory that is prominently stored in several major categories has considerable meaning and importance for the individual.*

Although other categories and subcategories exist in autobiographical memory, the categories detailed here appear to be the most important ones for exploring personality organization, identifying attitudes and expectations, and assessing major unresolved issues. Those who wish to study autobiographical memory for other reasons will want to consider the value of other categories and subcategories.

Once we understand how autobiographical memory is organized, it is much easier to explore. For instance, when we know that access to stored autobiographical memories is conditional upon a concordance with present mood, we can understand why a nondepressed person may not be able to recall any "sad" EMs. It is also easier to devise methods to access such memories. For instance, consider the following approach: "Think of the saddest event that you could possibly imagine. Are you feeling sad now? Now recall the events that made you feel saddest in your life." When the individual is able to experience a feeling of profound sadness, it is easier to access sad memories that would otherwise be blocked from awareness by a mood inconsistency.

WHAT COGNITIVE-PERCEPTUAL THEORY EXPLAINS

To explain human behavior, each theory of personality elects to focus on a particular aspect of human functioning. Once the point of reference is established, certain behaviors assume importance, and tools are developed to understand these behaviors. Psychoanalytic theory, for instance, is a mechanistic theory[1] that focuses on drives and drive reduction. The socially unacceptable nature of sexual drives made it difficult for Freud to study them directly. Freud chose instead to study those behaviors that reveal most clearly how these drives operate. He pioneered the use of free associations and dream material for this purpose. Social learning theorists, by contrast, study behaviors of interest and work backwards to determine what is reinforcing or rewarding these behaviors. For instance, if a child misbehaves in school, a social learning theorist seeks to determine what in the child's environment may be reinforcing this behavior.

Cognitive-Perceptual theory is a contextual theory that emphasizes a person's innate need to grow and extend his or her range of competence. The CP model is concerned with how this process becomes derailed and what can be done to facilitate growth. The existence of a need to grow is evident early in human development—from the infant who repetitively practices grasping objects in the crib, to the toddler who tirelessly perfects the skill of standing up and walking, to the two year old who informs his mother, "Me do myself." Social variables also influence the expression of this need. The child who identifies with strong, competent role models is more motivated to extend the range of his competence than the child who lacks such role models. Since life does not deal the same hand to each of us and since we are not endowed with the same innate abilities, the resulting combination of genetics, environment, and differences in motivation interact to produce a full range of human functioning from the profoundly retarded or psychotic (highly dysfunctional) to the highly functional. To understand the kind of issues that may compromise an individual's developmental progress, CP theory looks to the products of autobiographical memory for clues as to the nature and cause of the individual's life problems. Early memories can be used to identify major unresolved issues that are currently in process that have stymied the individual's ability to develop. By contrast, psychoanalytic methods (free associations especially) work best for the careful archeological digging and screening (microanalysis) associated with trying to understand the complex dance of drive and defense, as well as reconstructing the history that culminated in the analysand and becoming who he or she is today. As employed by CP theory, EMs help to determine where on the developmental track the individual's progress has been derailed and what can be done to correct the matter.

THE PREMISES OF COGNITIVE-PERCEPTUAL THEORY

Cognitive-Perceptual theory is founded on a set of assumptions regarding human behavior, just as Freud began with certain assumptions in formulating psychoanalytic theory. Psychoanalytic theory views all human beings as biological creatures impelled by certain drives. Freud was specifically interested in sexual and aggressive drives. He argued that because everyone has the same drives, human behavior is largely biologically determined. The only differences among people, according to Freudian theory, involve how they handle their instinctual drives, not whether they have them. By the same token, all individuals—whether

Austrians or aborigines—pass through the same psychosexual stages, which, Freud observed, are also biologically determined.

The foundation of CP theory also requires a set of assumptions regarding the nature of human beings. CP theory is primarily grounded in psychology, not biology. CP theory is concerned with an individual's needs, as opposed to drives. Individuals typically demonstrate a wide variety of needs, which are played out in different strengths. Some youngsters, for example, play basketball for hours. Others enjoy a game or two but quickly satisfy their need to compete and achieve—at least through this particular vehicle. Others evidence no need to play basketball and otherwise show a low need for achievement, mastery, and competition in other activities. CP theory is concerned with those psychological aspects that make each individual unique and different, whereas id-psychology focuses on those biological aspects of human functioning that make us alike.

Cognitive-Perceptual theory holds that autobiographical memory is an excellent tool for understanding the individual's unique way of constructing himself, others, and the world around him. If we want to understand how an individual perceives his world, the royal road to his internal organizational scheme (to coin a phrase) is autobiographical memory. As we perceive, so also do we remember. And vice versa.

THE COGNITIVE-PERCEPTUAL MODEL IN OVERVIEW

The description of the Cognitive-Perceptual model that follows has been revised and expanded from earlier papers (Bruhn, 1984, 1985; Bruhn & Bellow, 1984, 1987; Bruhn & Last, 1982). The following paragraph will explain, in overview, how the model operates; thereafter, key elements of the model will be defined and later discussed as a series of interrelated propositions.

According to the Cognitive-Perceptual model, perception aims for a "general impression" rather than a detailed picture of whole, a point made long ago by Bartlett (1932). The basis of selectivity in perception is that needs, fears, interests, and major beliefs direct and orchestrate first the perceptual process and later the reconstruction of the events which are recalled. The individual's needs, fears, interests, and major beliefs constitute his frame of reference. The frame of reference operates in present time and is revised to accommodate learning and novel experiences that cannot be accounted for in memory by existing schema. Schema, a term that relates to memory structure, can be described as expectations, rules or axioms derived from past experience that the individual maintains about himself, others, and the world. Memory primarily consists of schema about the world, rather than traces or images of the world. Attitudes derived from past experience endure in longer-term autobiographical memory rather than a heavy loading of factual information. The process of justification operates to help the individual construct events from memory so that the "factual details" mesh with the attitude that initially emerges in the recollective process. In sum, the Cognitive-Perceptual model utilizes a perception-memory-perception feedback loop in which the perception of the world is held to be constant unless anomalous experiences occur that have sufficient psychological impact to challenge the schemas which the individual maintains about his world. When these schemas change, the perceptual process accommodates itself to the new world view. It is hypothesized that parallel shifts in long-term memory then take place, consistent with the adaptive function of memory and the principle of utility.

A MAJOR UNRESOLVED ISSUE DEFINED

The Cognitive-Perceptual model holds that long-term autobiographical memory is organized following adaptive principles. That is, information that helps the individual to function more effectively is given prominence. One example is information that is relevant to gratifying major needs. A second example is data that pertains to important needs that are often frustrated. Prominent needs are inadequately gratified because the individual has not been able to develop the skills or coping strategies necessary to gratify these needs. Such deficits are linked to issues that are in process for the individual.

All individuals have issues in process—that is, issues currently being worked on. For some, the issues are not particularly troublesome. Consider, for example, assertiveness. Some successful, well-functioning individuals experience no difficulty with assertiveness except in isolated circumstances—for example, when dealing with individuals who are extremely powerful or with their most intimate relationships. Individuals with severe assertiveness problems, however, experience difficulties across a broad spectrum of situations, including, for instance, an activity as seemingly innocuous as ordering a cup of coffee. *An issue in process may involve a relatively small, delimited area of dysfunction, or it may implicate broad areas of functioning that make significant life progress impossible.* In either case, an unresolved issue is conceptualized and defined from a *contextual* framework.

Individuals who present clinically are usually caught up in a major unresolved issue that has stalemated further progress in their lives. Typically, problems with a major unresolved issue (*a*) have caused secondary effects (*b*, *c*, and *d*) that are unrelated to one another other than by association to *a*; or *a* has caused difficulties with *b*, which in turn has led to problems with *c*, which has caused problems with *d*; or some combination of the two. One of the clinician's first tasks is to conceptualize the interrelationship among the various issues that the client presents so as to understand cause and effect in the clinical picture.

The major unresolved issue is the one at the beginning of the causal chain. Such a determination can eventually be made in the process of psychotherapy, but to save time, the clinician can usually make the same determination from a brief set of spontaneous EMs (see Chapter 4), or from a set of autobiographical memories (see Chapter 5). To provide a brief illustration here, we will consider a young man who presents with relational difficulties. He complains that whenever he begins a relationship, everything goes well for a while, and then his womanfriend leaves him. He sees the pattern, but does not know how to change it and seeks help. An analysis of his spontaneous EMs reveals several EMs that focus on being disappointed by women. Later EMs suggest that disappointment and mistrust lead to withdrawal and that isolation leads to depression and self-deprecation. The major unresolved issue in this case (*a*) appears to be his ability to trust women. How the clinician chooses to deal with this issue depends upon his judgment regarding the type of intervention to which his client is most likely to respond. If he believes that his client cannot handle a direct approach, he will start at the end of the causal chain (self-deprecation and depression) and perhaps use anti-depressants and a simple form of cognitive therapy. If he believes that the client can tolerate a more powerful intervention, he may begin with his client's mistrust of women—how that came to be and how the client currently constructs his relationships with females. Perhaps there were modeling/identification aspects ("Dad didn't trust women either") or perhaps something occurred to alter the family's situation (as a first-born child, he was overthrown by a younger sister whom he perceived as his father's favorite).

The following can be said about major unresolved issues:

1. Major unresolved issues can be identified from an individual's spontaneous EMs.

2. The existence of a major unresolved issue is considered part of the normal development process and is not, by itself, a sign of psychopathology. A major unresolved issue can reflect an age-appropriate developmental issue or a chronic, entrenched problem that is developmentally inappropriate. Many normally developing latency-aged boys, for instance, recall "motor memories"—such as riding a bicycle for the first time—that reflect normal mastery or achievement issues appropriate to latency age.

3. Pathological major unresolved issues may be distinguished from non-pathological issues in that individuals with the former are usually

"stuck" to a greater degree—they have not been able to progress and their issues are usually not age-appropriate.

4. When a major unresolved issue has been resolved, the individual's spontaneous EMs will change to reflect the next major unresolved issue in procress.

MAJOR PROPOSITIONS

Cognitive-Perceptual theory can be reduced to a small number of key propositions:

1. Perception is selective, not photographic. This principle owes its empirical roots to Bartlett's (1932) impressive experimental demonstrations. The bases for selection in perception are fears, needs, interests, and major beliefs.

Before the turn of the century, William James (1890) made a similar point:

> Millions of items of the outward order are present to my senses which never properly enter into my experience. Why? Because they have no *interest* for me.... Only those items which I *notice* shape my mind—without selective interest, experience is an utter chaos. Interest alone gives accent and emphasis, light and shade, background and foreground—intelligible perspective in a word. (p. 402)

In 1913, Schrecker presented a paper on memory selectivity and proposed that memory is

> a construction, a fiction ... [but] one may not assert that a childhood recollection, because it is a construction, is useless.... To the contrary ... by understanding this construction the individual shows that he attributes to its content a certain importance for his development.... Thus we obtain the most important means ... for understanding the present situation of this individual. (pp. 147–148)

Dreikurs (1923/1950) continued this theme:

> The earliest memories of childhood are always significant.... The dynamics of memory explain the fact that we choose to remember from the thousands of experiences of our early childhood only

those which fit in our general—and still present—outlook on life. These early recollections, therefore, are indicative of our life style.

Pear (1922) went a step further, proposing that both perception and later recollections are selective, and that the basis for the selective process is determined by an individual's personality. Bartlett (1932) empirically demonstrated how an individual's frame of reference influences perception and recall. He found subjects' reproductions of simple stories were altered to conform with "the temperament, or the character, of the person who effects the recall" (p. 213). Since verbatim recall rarely occurred, Bartlett posited that memory reorganization and change are the rule rather than the exception. He suggested individuals actively and creatively construct a memory; they do not merely reproduce the past.

Bartlett (1932) contradicted the trace theory popular at the time and proposed that the mind was composed of schemas, which are abstractions or simplifications of past experience. Serving as an apperceptive screen, these schemas bias perception, accentuating certain details while minimizing others. Schemas also organize recall, frequently resulting in highly personalized reconstructions of the past. Thus, the perception-recall process rarely produces a literal or precise memory. Instead, perceptions are generally vague, with specific details added in accordance with their attitudes, interests, and affects.

Stern (1938) suggested emotional factors selectively influence remembering. Similarly, Gordon (1937) and Edwards (1942) proposed that an individual's current needs transform perception and memory, leading to enhanced recall of experiences corresponding with the present frame of reference.

Rapaport (1942/1971) argued in addition that "memory processes are subject to the activity of selective forces related to deep strata of the personality and the field conditions under which registration and remembering take place and which exist in the retention period" (p. 136).

Using Bartlett's (1932) concept of schema, Schachtel (1947) offered a developmental explanation of the distortion and biases observed in adults' perception and recall. He proposed that young children encode events in a form incompatible with cognitive schemas developed in adulthood. Given this dissimilarity between child and adult cognitive structures, adults have difficulty effectively retrieving childhood memories. Preverbal experiences are discontinuous with mature, conventional ways of experiencing the world. Thus, adults cannot recapture or accurately remember this early state of being. Instead, present needs, fears, and interests bias and distort adults' reconstructions of the past.

In a further expansion of Bartlett's (1932) theory, Neisser (1982) proposed that attention and perception, like recall, are constructive processes in which adaptive variation is the rule. Seeing, hearing, and remembering all reconstruct the past, organizing around an individual's subjective cognitive structures, or schemas. While these schemas facilitate recall, they also distort both initial construction (perception) and later reconstruction (recall).

2. The individual's frame of reference can be conceptualized as those aspects of experience that merit attention, including those associated with needs, fears, interests, and major beliefs. An Eskimo, for example, differentiates many varieties of snow, as indicated by unique words for each variety, whereas a Floridian may only differentiate snow from sleet. Making clear differentiations among types of snow has an adaptive value for Eskimos that it does not obtain for Floridians. The Eskimo schema for snow accordingly exhibits a complexity lacking in the equivalent schema for Floridians.

The individual's frame of reference operates in present time and is broadened to accommodate new interests, novel experiences, and changes in perspective.

3. Schemas regarding the self, others, and world are subject to change when present experience is both anomalous and sufficiently powerful to render existing schemas obsolete.

Schemas are general rules, derived from past experience, about what can be expected from others and the world, as well as how the self is expected to function in relation to both. Schemas determine whether we perceive data as meriting attention. If there is no schema for the perceptual data being scanned, it is unlikely that we will process it unless life experience provides a compelling reason. From daily experience we constantly develop, test, change, and discard hypotheses about the nature of our world. Schemas can be changed in several ways. For example, a child who has always had positive experiences with furry animals but is nipped by a fluffy dog is likely to approach dogs differently before and after the experience of being bitten. Her expectations associated with the schema of dogs have changed.

A clinical example also comes to mind. A husband perceived his wife, who evidenced many signs of compulsive behavior, as not loving him (his schema of her) because she frequently refused to have sex with him, which he held to be part of her wifely duties. His reasoning process can be summarized as follows: "If she loved me, then making love with me would be a priority when she knows that is something I want. But because she makes dusting, vacuuming, etc., a priority and is always 'too busy,' she must care little about me or my feelings. Therefore, she must not love me." His wife's view was quite different. She felt intimidated by the intensity of her husband's sexual drive. She was confident about her ability to do housework, but she was very uncertain about her ability to satisfy his sexual needs. When he realized that his wife had a problem— that she was afraid of failing as a sexual partner and therefore avoided sexual situations—his perception of her changed and their long-standing sexual problems were reprocessed as "something she needed help with." His schema of his wife ("she does not love me") changed once he understood that she was preoccupied with failing and being rejected.

4. Memory consists of schemas about the world rather than traces or images of the world.

Eidetic (photographic) memory is the exception rather than the rule in long-term memory. By its very nature, photographic memory is bulky and inefficient, since it requires too much cortical storage space. The need for efficient cognitive processing places severe constraints on the amount of information that can be stored. For instance, to study effectively for a college physics exam, a student must make decisions about what information is important and organize the course material so that the most important data (laws, formulas, definitions) can be readily accessed.

5. What endures in memory are attitudes derived from past experience rather than a heavy loading of factual information.

What the individual constructs from having been bitten by a dog, for example, is more important than the fact of being bitten. One individual may conclude that she should not try to pet snarling dogs, whereas another may decide that all dogs are dangerous and should be avoided. The principle of attraction determines which events will be recalled from long-term memory. If an individual perceives himself as a victim, he will recall events from long-term memory consistent with that perception. Events in autobiographical memory that have incorporated similar attitudes—at the time or retrospectively—are infused with energy from current perceptions and attitudes so that what is recalled mirrors current perceptions. This phenomenon can be readily demonstrated from clinical experience. For instance, a client who is suffering an acute depressive episode will report EMs that reflect his current pessimistic outlook. Moreover, his memories will depict the unresolved issue most closely associated with his present depressive episode. The principle of attraction determines which events are energized and pulled from autobiographical memory so that the past and current experience present a coherent, internally consistent picture to the individual.

6. Cognitive-Perceptual theory posits that early memories reflect current perceptions, consistent with the principle of attraction.

We recall incidents that mirror and substantiate our current perceptions and beliefs and "overlook" or "forget" incidents that are inconsistent with present beliefs. For didactic purposes, let us deny the principle of attraction and argue the following two propositions in turn:

1. That which is recalled from autobiographical memory is the antithesis of present perceptions and beliefs.
2. That which is recalled from autobiographical memory is uncorrelated with present perceptions and beliefs—that is, some beliefs are consistent with present perceptions and beliefs, and an equivalent number are opposed.

These two competing propositions exhaust the logical alternatives concerning the relationship between early memories and present beliefs and perceptions. Consider the first possibility. If EMs contained only perceptions and beliefs that directly oppose present perceptions and beliefs, the world would be a confusing place indeed. Every present belief would be contradicted by past experience. How could learning take place under such circumstances, and how could memory have adaptive value?

The second proposition is that present perceptions and beliefs are not correlated with those found in early memories. Such a memory system would presuppose minimal organization and no utility. If memory weighted equally a full spectrum of contradicting opinions about the world, the result would be total cognitive chaos. With such a system, lions might be alternatively perceived as dangerous or cuddly, with no sense of contradiction registering between the two perceptions. Such a system would lack adaptive value.

It is intuitively obvious that memory must be organized so that data about the world is consistent and coherent, as opposed to inconsistent, incoherent, or random. Without such organization, we would have no basis for responding adaptively to the wide variety of situations that present themselves in our lives.

Having demonstrated that memory must reflect and substantiate current perceptions and beliefs, we can readily deduce what must happen when present perceptions and beliefs change by psychotherapy, learning, or other means. When schemas associated with present perceptions and beliefs change, existing memories must be modified to reflect these changes, or they must disappear from consciousness. Alternatively, "new" memories, which were previously unavailable to consciousness, may surface, consistent with the principle of attraction.

7. The process of justification regulates the reconstruction of events from long-term memory so that "factual details" are consistent with the attitude that initially emerges in the recollective process.

Current attitudes are a major source of distortions in memory and perceptions. Our attitudes interfere with the processing of any perceptual data that is discordant with our beliefs. For instance, an individual who expects to be victimized by others will process good treatment differently than an individual who expects to be treated fairly. Once an expectation is solidly in place—especially if it assumes the status of an axiom—only powerful disconfirmatory experiences can change these expectations. As used here, expectations are hypotheses or probability statements born of personal experience, whereas axioms are firmly established beliefs that have assumed a status equivalent to physical laws (e.g., the law of gravity).

As used in CP theory, axioms are expectations associated with major beliefs or conclusions that an individual has reached about himself, others, or the world around him. In contrast to how the term is used in formal logic, axioms in autobiographical memory deal with constructions, "emotional givens," or subjective truths that are not called into question under ordinary circumstances. Depending upon its centrality to the core of personality structure, a particular axiom may play a fundamental role in personality organization and self-concept. Consider, for example, a hard-working, responsible, first-born son whose mother devoted the majority of her time to her youngest son, who was constantly in trouble. The first son can process this dynamic in a multitude of ways, including, "I am not lovable. Nothing that I do is enough to gain my mother's attention and love, so the problem must be a basic flaw in me. This flaw has made me unlovable." If this construction assumes the status of an "emotional given" or an axiom, it will take an extraordinary event(s) to invalidate it. The individual will develop a depressive core, including a pervasive sense of futility and hopelessness: "There is nothing I can do. . . ." If, however, the original experiential basis for this axiom can be uncovered and successfully challenged—the individual's belief that even his ne'er-do-well brother was favored over him—profound changes in personality organization can take place. An analog for axioms in personality organization is a cornerstone in a building. If this load-bearing element is seriously compromised, the building may collapse. Similarly, once a major axiom is successfully challenged, the personality structure that has developed around it will also be undermined.

8. Memory targets data for storage that has the greatest potential adaptive value.

Memory was not designed as a depository for useless information. We recall what we do for a reason, and that reason, ultimately, is to maintain or increase our level of adaptability. Useless data (e.g., nonsense syllables) is quickly forgotten, even when learned and stored in long-term memory, because no purpose is served in retaining it. Much of what is recalled from autobiographical memory is associated with the satisfaction or frustration of the individual's major needs. Each individual maintains a personal hierarchy of needs, which can be deduced from an analysis of memory content, particularly of EMs, which are more selective.

9. Memory is organized according to the adaptive principle of utility. That which is perceived as most useful is highlighted, energized, and raised to a position of prominence in long-term memory.

Consider the example of two high school boys studying for an English exam. One aspires to be a writer and is therefore highly motivated. He is interested in the process of character development and how one develops tension in a story, thereby holding reader interest. The other is motivated only to pass so that he can retain his driving privileges. The second boy sees little intrinsic value in what he learns. He perceives the course material as having only *instrumental* value—that is, learning enough to pass the exam permits him to continue driving his car. The first boy, however, perceives the material as intrinsically useful and is motivated to learn it. The teacher has stressed character development in his literary selections, class lectures, and discussions. The first youngster expects a high intrinsic payoff for what he studies, apart from whether he does well on his exam. What remains prominent in long-term memory for both boys after exams are over relates to the *perceived intrinsic value* of the material that has been learned. Several months later, the first boy will likely demonstrate excellent recall because the material held intrinsic interest for him; the second boy will likely quickly forget what he learned because he studied primarily to retain his driving privileges. What is remembered and raised to a position of prominence in long-term memory is material that has value.

Because EMs are part of long-term memory and conform to the same principle of utility, we can similarly assume that all childhood recollections have intrinsic meaning and value to the individual today.

10. The contents of long-term autobiographical memory can be divided into two major categories:

   A. Negative affect memories that reflect the frustration of major needs; and

   B. Positive affect memories that depict the satisfaction of major needs.

Both categories contain data that has adaptive value. The first category reflects work in process, consistent with Gestalt principles. In classic German experiments from the 1920s and 1930s, school children were interrupted during their attempts to solve math problems. Results indicated that they were more likely to recall problems that they had not completed than those they had. Similarly, we are more likely to recall in autobiographical memory work in process—unfinished business—than memories involving previous life problems that present no current challenge. Negative affect EMs usually depict issues that lie at the cutting edge of development and represent "the next step" to be accomplished.

The second category—positive affect early memories—illustrates how the individual's major needs can best be satisfied. The individual who recalls a standing ovation at the conclusion of his performance at an elementary school play fondly remembers the gratification of strong exhibitionistic needs (see glossary of needs). The person who remembers a series of EMs involving birthdays and Christmases where he received special gifts evidences a strong narcissistic need to be treated as a special person. Positive affect memories serve a dual purpose:

1. They remind the individual of the kinds of situations that provide special satisfaction when major needs are gratified (orienting function); and

2. They help the individual to stabilize his mood by providing hope during frustrating moments when life is not going smoothly (stabilizing function).

Put in different terms, positive affect early memories express wishes, while negative affect EMs express fears, uncertainty or tension about issues in process. Operationally, memories can be identified as reflecting wishes or fears by asking the individual to identify the strongest feeling associated with his memory and to rate it on a 7 point scale (see Bruhn, 1989, *The Early Memories Procedure*, pp. 9 and 10). This system works well with individuals who are in touch with their feelings.

A COMMENT REGARDING THE MAJOR PROPOSITIONS

As formulated in this chapter, the Cognitive-Perceptual model considers the process of perception, the interaction between perception and memory, and the circumstances under which perceptions change. The model was presented in this fashion to provide a sharper focus to these volumes, which focus on EMs and their clinical use. If this were a strictly theoretical book, a broader theoretical perspective would have been adopted. We would have looked at infants and the genesis of perception and schemas, the rules that govern perception and how these rules change as a function of cognitive development, and the changing needs of the developing personality. In other words, we would merge concepts from perception and memory with what we know about cognitive development and developmentally based changes in needs to construct a robust and conceptually satisfying model of personality. Much of Piaget's work on cognitive development is philosophically and theoretically compatible with CP theory and can be readily assimilated. Erik Erickson's work on the stages of human development would be modified slightly to emphasize the developmental aspects of needs. For instance, an infant shows a developmentally appropriate need for succor, which must be satisfied so he can learn to depend on and trust others. As the infant moves into the toileting stage, he must learn to modulate his need for succor and learn to cooperate. At this time, parents attempt to establish a more realistic balance between giving and receiving, and the needs associated with both activities. A full elaboration of CP theory could be accomplished here, except that there is no reason to do so at this time. A knowledge of cognitive development and the ontogeny of changing developmental needs adds minimally to our understanding of EMs and autobiographical memory.

This chapter has attempted to establish the philosophical basis for a relatively new model of EM interpretation: the Cognitive-Perceptual model. The next chapter will demonstrate how this model can be used to analyze autobiographical memories.

NOTE

1. Pepper (1970), in his philosophical discussion of meta-theory in science, argues that four separate meta-theoretical types can be distinguished. Each meta-theory poses a unique view of the world. Each is philosophically distinct. Freudian theory would be described as a mechanistic theory in Pepper's system. CP theory is an excellent example of a contextual meta-theory. Contextual and mechanistic theories are philosophically incompatible in that each presents a unique view of human kind. Only models of the same type (e.g., two mechanistic models) can be compared and judged for adequacy using such standard criteria as parsimony and ability to make accurate predictions. Mechanistic and contextual meta-theories are structured so differently that they cannot be compared.

4

APPLYING THE COGNITIVE-PERCEPTUAL MODEL TO EARLY MEMORIES

Earliest memories are absolutely specific, distinctive and character-
istic for each individual; moreover, they reveal, probably more clearly
than any other single psychological datum, the central core of each
person's psychodynamics, his chief motivations, form of neurosis,
and emotional problem.

Saul, Snyder, and Sheppard (1956)

Early memories function like a *blueprint*: "This is who I am, this is how
others are, this is how I will be treated, this is what the world is like." Just
as the builder renders the architect's blueprint into a completed structure, so also do we replicate in our present lives the expectations, perceptions, and beliefs portrayed in our EMs. The present thus endlessly
repeats the form of what we recall from the past as long as the blueprint remains constant. Individuals who recall being rejected by a significant other
in their EMs are likely depressed now because they continue to experience
rejections from important persons in their lives by playing out the same maladaptive relational patterns that first caused them to be rejected. Unless the
individual has committed himself to a program of growth, the blueprint evident in his EMs will remain constant for many years until major life events
(loss of job, divorce, death of parents) force him to alter his coping strategies.
A tough taskmaster, change is not for the somnolent or faint of heart. It is
no wonder that early memories tend to remain stable for most adults, often
for five or ten years, sometimes for a lifetime.

Subsequent sections of this chapter will explore the preceding in
greater depth. We will look specifically at the relationship between trau-

mas and early memories, the value of EMs, the more common errors that clinicians make in the assessment of autobiographical memory, the interpretation of EMs, and the metaphorical quality of EMs. Memories from Dwight David Eisenhower, Golda Meir, Lee Iacocca, Mahatma Gandhi, and Bill Bradley will be used to illustrate various aspects of early memory interpretation.

TRAUMAS AND EARLY MEMORIES

Many professionals express reservations about working directly with early memories because they regard them as screens for traumatic events, which was Freud's position (1899/1950). Thus, they argue, the potential risk is too great. What if the material unduly upsets the client or, worse, triggers a psychotic episode? My opinion is that some EMs are "screen memories" consistent with Freud's description, but most are not. Most EMs deal not with manifestly innocuous data, as Freud argued, but with extremely significant material. Memories from Dwight David Eisenhower and Golda Meir, which will be presented later in the chapter, illustrate this point.

Let us discuss what we mean by the terms "trauma," "traumatic memory," and "repressed or unconscious traumatic memory." A trauma is an event that damaged the individual emotionally in some manner. The individual may or may not be consciously aware that a particular event traumatized him. Some individuals may be aware of how the experience affected them and will disclose this if asked. A traumatic memory refers to a memory of a traumatic event. Many traumatic memories are readily available to consciousness. In fact, often such memories may be partially or totally processed (reinterpreted from a contemporaneous viewpoint and worked through emotionally). The memories that present difficulties for clients are repressed or unconscious traumatic memories. Such memories are repressed and unconscious because the client is not prepared to deal with the material. Should such material emerge before the individual is emotionally prepared to process it, he may feel upset, overwhelmed and highly anxious. I do not ordinarily recommend persistent, intrusive probing to uncover such material. What the client can recall, he is ordinarily prepared to deal with. What has been repressed has been buried precisely because it is too overwhelming and painful to work through at that point in time. Should growth ensue that would permit exploration of such material, such memories often thrust themselves into awareness, much as rocks heave themselves up in New England soil during spring thaw.

In most cases, early memories are highly significant and often charged with affect as well. Working with such material, however, affords little risk to the client because these memories reflect current perceptions, attitudes, and work-in-process. Such memories are usually available to consciousness with minimal probing and are not deeply repressed. Occasional examples of Freud's innocuous screen memories present themselves in a clinical population, but these are relatively rare in a private outpatient population. It is only when the clinician attempts to uncover those memories that are deeply repressed by extensive use of free association and other extraordinary techniques that the client is in any jeopardy. Otherwise, it can be assumed that if a memory is readily available to consciousness, the client is prepared to process it.

EARLY MEMORIES HAVE VALUE

To the extent that long-term autobiographical memory conforms to the principle of adaptation, whatever is available to awareness must have value. A corollary to this principle is: the older the material, the more likely it is to be valuable. An analogy can be made between very old memories and sediment that has been sluiced from a gold miner's pan. The more times that worthless material has been washed from the pan, the more likely what remains is gold.

It is intuitively obvious that data preserved from early childhood must be significant due to its rarity. The rarity of early events can be demonstrated experientially. Begin by reconstructing the specific events (happenings, conversations, etc.) of yesterday. After some systematic probing (What did I do at work? Where did I eat lunch? Who did I talk to on the phone? What did I watch on television?), you will probably reconstruct a fairly accurate, detailed record.

Now do the same for a week ago yesterday; a month ago yesterday; a year ago yesterday; ten years ago yesterday. If you are like most people, the amount of data from each time period will decrease rapidly until it asymptotically approaches zero, especially with regard to specific events. You may be able to recall the name of your second grade teacher and where you lived, but it will be difficult to recall many specific events from that year, particularly from a randomly selected day in that year (see Figure 1.1).

How can we understand this phenomenon? We are obviously dealing with a normal forgetting curve, but to label a phenomenon does not explain it. After a few moments of introspection, we may conclude that long-term memory is not organized to recall significant events by dates, with a few exceptions—Christmases, birthdays, anniversaries, and the like. Normally, such an organization scheme—for example, Wednesdays—has little adaptive value. But beyond this, as we proceed ever back in time, the probability that a particular thought, concept, or experience will have enduring adaptive value to us today approaches zero. This, too, seems intuitively obvious, but what is the explanation? Consider the experience of a ten-year-old boy. Why would it be important for the man, thirty years later, to recall the subtleties of marble playing; how it felt to play his third season of little league baseball; and what his attitudes were toward presidential politics? How many of us can recall as children how we used to understand politics or government functioning? There is so much from the past that, memorially speaking, is useless clutter and needs to be pitched out, much as we need to purge our houses each spring.

The probability that any random childhood event will be spontaneously recalled approaches zero precisely because memory conforms to the principle of adaptation. Most childhood events are not especially significant, at least not from our vantage point as adults. On the other hand, one must suspect that any event which is recalled must be particularly significant. In part this is true because autobiographical memory functions adaptively. Anything left after so many iterations of "pitching out" must have more enduring value than the events of yesterday, for example. The vast majority of recent events will be forgotten within a year while our same early memories are infinitely more likely to be recalled from long-term memory a year hence. Although the preceding makes sense conceptually, it can also be tested empirically as is so with any scientific hypothesis.

COMMON MISUNDERSTANDINGS ABOUT LONG-TERM AUTOBIOGRAPHICAL MEMORY

Most psychologists and mental health professionals misapprehend in several crucial respects how long-term autobiographical memory functions. These misunderstandings result in predictable errors that affect how memories are interpreted. Let us consider several of the more common errors.

First, there is the misapprehension that all EMs, directly or indirectly, involve traumas. This error is a legacy from classical psychoanalysis. The core belief is that an emotionally devastating event occurred in early childhood that flooded and overwhelmed the individual's defenses, causing serious and likely irreparable emotional damage. Freud believed that such memories are often partially removed from awareness through what he termed a screen memory. He held that the original trauma could often be uncovered by a process of free associations. Freud's error was to take a small subset of EMs that are just as he described and to generalize to EMs as a group. That is, if some EMs involve traumatic events (a true statement), all must involve either traumatic events or events that function as screens for traumatic events (a false statement). I have collected EMs from several thousand individuals and seen perhaps a thousand more for assessment and/or therapy. Although estimates are hazardous, I would guess that perhaps ninety-five percent of all spontaneous EMs from a wide cross-section of individuals are not particularly traumatic. They instead reflect major life interests and preoccupations, key perceptions, and important expectations as well as the individual's most significant attitudes and current world view.

Second, there is the belief that childhood traumas have caused us to be what we are today. Put another way, this is the error of determinism. The core belief regarding human nature from Freud's perspective is that human beings are capable of growth for only a brief period of time, that most growth takes place in the first two to three years of life, and that by age eight or so the plasticity of personality that permits change to occur is no more. Thus, to talk to a strict Freudian about change in adulthood is like discussing whether it would be possible for a seagull to become a hummingbird. Early memories from a Freudian perspective become the surviving debris of ancient catastrophes—a distorted record of events that unleashed terrible and irreparable devastation.

The error in deterministic thinking is the same type of error that exists with traumas. Freud's position is correct for some individuals. Some individuals suffer terrible traumas early in life, and many are never able to transcend these effects. This is most likely to be true in the case of severely disturbed individuals, and these were the patients Freud tended to work with. Most individuals who are not severely disturbed, however, are not so rigidly set in their basic characters that they cannot change if they are sufficiently motivated to do so.

Early memories typically reflect the product of a creative process within the self, not traumas. The creation of the EM begins with what might be called the core. An example might be an individual's sense of weakness and vulnerability and accompanying need for security and succor. The core of the memory is associated with a major unresolved issue, or what has been described as the individual's major unfinished business (see Bruhn & Bellow, 1984). In the present case, the unfinished business is associated with the individual's feeling of inadequacy. Once the unfinished business is established as a priority, an event is creatively selected from long-term memory to depict that issue. An example would be an individual who recalled tripping on a stick, skinning his knee, and running home crying for his mother. This memory expresses the individual's perception of himself as inadequate, of the world as dangerous, and of his resulting need for security and succor. If hieroglyphics are pictographs, EMs become "perceptographs," or ways of symbolically depicting important perceptual schemas under the guise of depicting actual historical events.

Last, there is the misapprehension that EMs comprise an historical record and, as such, are correct in most major respects. This fallacy leads us into many problems—not just in treating clients but in understanding ourselves.

Although some individuals recall events more accurately than others, strict veridicality is an illusion. This can be easily demonstrated by several techniques. First, relate a brief story to an individual and have him convey it to a second person who will relate it to a third person who will tell it to a fourth. The story that the fifth person recounts probably will not be recognizable from the original. Bartlett's (1932) pioneering work contains ample evidence that memory is usually not photographic and that specific memories are far more often a matter of construction than exact reproduction. This premise can be proven by the following experiment. Begin by writing down your first three EMs. Next, describe how you view the scenes in the EMs. Are you looking down at yourself from above in the memory? Or are you literally seeing yourself doing something or interacting with others from a perspective that places you outside your body? If either is true, you have demonstrated that your EMs must be constructions (see Chapter 1). How else could you see yourself in the EM? Only if you see the scene now as you originally saw it—for example, through the eyes of a two year old and from the same perspective—is there any possibility that the memory is a reproduction of the original event (see Milton Erickson's EMs later in this chapter and note type 1 EMs in Chapter 5).

The role and function of autobiographical memory is understood by few clinicians, and as a result errors occur in the handling of material attributed to a client's early life. A better understanding of autobiographical memory will help minimize these errors.

ELICITING ORAL EARLY MEMORIES

Previously, recommendations were given (Bruhn, 1984) for eliciting oral EMs. There are two circumstances in which a clinician might ordinarily obtain a set of EMs:

1. As part of a psychological test battery; or
2. As part of the intake process.

Under ordinary circumstances, it is recommended that a full set of memories be obtained in writing via the Early Memories Procedure (EMP) (see Chapter 5). However, there are occasions at intake when it is necessary to obtain a sample of oral EMs because a full EMP may not be practical—for instance, if the client is too scattered, unfocused, or depressed to work on his own. For those situations, a slightly modified version of the EMP directions is recommended:

Think back to the earliest memory you have of a specific happening or event from your childhood. Choose an event that you actually remember. For instance, leave out incidents someone told you about that you do not actually recall. Also, be sure that it is a one time event of the form, "I remember one time...." Describe it in as much detail as your recollection of the event permits.

In addition, the following probes are used for the first memory:

— What is the clearest part of the memory?

— What is the strongest feeling in the memory? What thought or action is this connected with?

— What was your approximate age at the time of the memory?

If EMs are used as part of a psychological test battery, it is recommended that the EMP either be given in advance to the client or, if this is not possible, that the EMP be introduced at the end of the assessment session with a stamped, self-addressed manila envelope for its return. If the client is not a good candidate for the EMP, I usually request EMs last, after the battery is otherwise complete. This battery, for adults, typically consists of the Bender Gestalt and retest, Human Figure Drawings, Kinetic Family Drawing, Wechsler Adult Intelligence Scale (Revised), Rorschach, Thematic Apperception Test, EMs, and possibly an MMPI or another computer-scored test. Thus, two short-term memory tasks (Bender retest from memory and Digit Span on the Wechsler) have already been completed. The instructions for the EMs test when taken following a psychological assessment are:

You have already completed two memory tests: memory for designs and memory for numbers. These were tests of short-term memory. Now I am going to ask that you work on a long-term memory task with me. [The purpose of this introduction is to distract the subject from the projective nature of the task by inducing a set to "remember all that he can," just as he did with the designs and numbers.]

I am interested in your earliest memories, the earliest events you can recall.

I have found that some people recall a great deal from their early life. They can remember back to the time when they were very, very small. And some people recall these events in great detail. It is as if they are watching a movie of what happened to them, or in some cases re-experiencing these events just as they occurred. Some people hear things that occurred in these events, much like a sound track from a movie. Some can recall feeling certain things or smelling certain smells or touching certain things, and in some cases very vividly, as if they had just happened or were happening now. For others, the events are not as vivid. In some cases, they may seem rather blurry or indistinct; in other cases, the individual may recall that something occurred without being able to visualize it in his mind's eye. Some people have many, many memories, even from very early in their lives. Others recall much less, and sometimes only from their later childhood, from ages six or seven or even later. Now I'd like you to tell me the earliest memory of a specific event that you can recall from your childhood. Describe what you recall in as much detail as you can.

These instructions are designed to engage the subject's curiosity about himself and his memory processes. Thus, he tends to focus not on "What do I recall?" but rather on "How do I recall what I recall?" Anxiety is minimized by these instructions. The subject does not have to worry about what the examiner will think of his productions; he has been told in advance that every possible outcome is acceptable.

It is recommended that the following free association instructions be given for the second EM: "What early memory comes to mind next? This may be chronologically the next early memory or simply another early memory that comes to mind." The standard probes (clearest part? strongest feeling? age?) follow when the client is finished describing each memory. The instructions for the third and subsequent EMs are the same: "What early memory comes to mind next?" The clinician may stop when it appears that the client is running out of material.

If the clinician wishes to assess the whole of autobiographical memory, the following probe is recommended: "Previously, you have described experiences from your early childhood. Now, think about memories that you have from your entire life. These incidents may be very early or more recent. Choose one that is especially vivid or particularly important to you for whatever reason." Again, the three standard probes apply to this memory.

Obtaining a set of oral EMs is a straightforward process in most cases. If any difficulties arise, they are likely to pertain to the following:

1. The client claims he cannot recall any memories; or
2. The client gives memories of a repeated event—for example, "We always used to have a picnic after church in the summer...."

In the first case, it is recommended that the clinician employ positive suggestions: "Sometimes it takes time for something to come to mind ...relax and take your time... perhaps it would be easier to begin with something not so early." Resist the urge to prompt or structure: "Maybe you can remember something about your mother...school...friends." Such probes change the nature of the task from eliciting spontaneous EMs to obtaining directed memories (see Part II of the EMP, Chapter 5).

In the case of the client who persists in giving reports or pattern memories (memories of repeated events), the following may help to get him back on track: "Is this a memory that you have of a specific event, something that happened one time?" It is important to obtain specific EMs since pattern memories differ in several crucial respects from one-time memories. For instance, they tend to be disproportionately positive and they probably serve a different ecological function—to stabilize one's mood. Other differences between EMs of specific events and pattern memories will be discussed in the research literature Volume II.

EARLY MEMORIES AS PERCEPTOGRAPHS

Humans have created many systems to communicate. The most common is spoken language. Next, there is written language, which either tries to symbolically capture sounds or attempts to schematically depict words or concepts (hieroglyphics). Other systems include body or sign language (signing for the deaf), flags (navy, coast guard), smoke signals (Native Americans), and binary computer language.

As a language system, early memories can be described as *perceptographs*. A perceptograph communicates concepts through visually encoded schemas. EMs play out concepts symbolically by drawing on purported historical events from life experience. Whether historically accurate or unconsciously fabricated, these memories depict issues that have special contemporary relevance: issues in process. Such memories are unconsciously selected, following the principle of attraction, to remind the self of unfinished business having great current relevance.

The violent psychopath is likely to recall violence in his EMs, the victim being victimized. The depressed person will recall the symbolic basis for his depression (losses, failures), while the anxious individual will recall the situations that are most likely to produce anxiety. So it is that our present fantasies, preoccupations, and fears will draw from the deepest recesses of autobiographical memory those events that play out unresolved issues that are primary for us now. In this respect, EMs function much like a daytimer—to remind us of our current priorities in the area of personal growth.

As is true of any language system, EMs adhere to a set of rules or principles. These principles are outlined below:

1. The earlier the EM, the more selective the selection process. As we proceed further back in time, we remember less. Thus, the pool of

available EMs from which we select progressively diminishes until by age 2, 3, 4, or 5 we have access to an extremely small pool of EMs—typically around 1 to 5.

2. Since experience per unit time is approximately constant over time, what survives from the tens of thousands of events from early childhood is particularly important. If one incident survives from the first five years of life, we must ask, "why this particular incident of all the events that occurred?"

3. Memory conforms to the principles of utility and adaptation—in other words, we remember what has value for us and what makes us functional and competent. We quickly forget information that we consider useless.

4. Just as memory conforms to the principles of utility and adaptation, so do EMs, which are regulated by the same principles that regulate memory.

5. Unusually clear EMs, or parts of EMs, are clear because they are particularly important. Clarity in memories is analogous to highlighting parts of a college text. Highlighting such material causes it to stand out. Clear EMs stand out because they draw more psychic energy than comparable memories. This process occurs because the individual recognizes at a deeper level that this material is important and must be processed.

6. Particularly negative EMs that are also clear are more likely to contain the most important unresolved issue. Extremely negative EMs are usually unpleasant for one or more of the following reasons:

   A. A very strong need has been frustrated;

   B. An important coping skill (assertiveness, self-disclosure) is deficient, or missing entirely, which in turn causes the individual to suffer disappointment, anxiety, humiliation, and the like;

   C. A major axiom (key attitude) functions to cause the individual to behave in a self-defeating manner.
      Example: A key axiom ("women will humiliate you") sabotages the individual's attempt to establish intimate relationships with women. The negative affect in the EM functions as a signal to alert the individual to unfinished business in the EMs. The basis (frustrated need, deficient coping skills, maladaptive axiom) for the problem is likely to be played out in the EM.

7. Particularly positive EMs that are also clear are more likely to depict the satisfaction of needs that are strong for the individual. These EMs, which function as wishes (a strong need has been gratified), usually emerge to orient the individual toward situations in her or his life that have special meaning. Often, these situations do not

turn out as consistently positively as the individual would like or they are not as frequent. The EMs remind her or him of an important issue in process that has only been partly resolved.

8. We tend to focus selectively on a small handful of unresolved issues in our EMs because it is adaptive to do so. To focus on a full range of unresolved issues would be counterproductive as most of us would feel overwhelmed.

9. EMs introduce only the unresolved issues that we are currently prepared to process. The issues that we are not prepared to process are embedded in EMs that are not available to the consciousness— what Freud described as traumatic, repressed memories.

10. When an issue is resolved, our EMs change to reflect the emergence of a new set of unresolved issues. Retaining a set of obsolete axioms, attitudes, and schemas in our EMs would violate one of the most basic principles of memory functioning: longterm memory does not retain antiquated attitudes and useless information. To paraphrase one memory researcher, it is difficult to remember what you used to believe.

INTERPRETING EARLY MEMORIES WITH THE COGNITIVE-PERCEPTUAL METHOD

Several papers have previously illustrated the interpretation of EMs with the Cognitive-Perceptual method, including analyses of Eisenhower's first memory (Bruhn & Bellow, 1984), Golda Meir's EMs (Bruhn & Bellow, 1987) and several clinical cases (Bruhn, 1984, 1985). This section will provide a brief introduction to CP techniques.

Cognitive-Perceptual theory focuses on perceptions, needs, interests, wishes, fears, expectations, major beliefs, and unresolved issues in early memories. The question is how best to extract this data from EMs.

Through a process of trial and error, I found that the most effective starting place is "precis" work. As defined by Webster, a precis is a concise summary of essential points, statements or facts. From the standpoint of CP theory, a precis attempts to uncover the basic structure of a memory, the form or skeleton that is embellished by details of the memory. The precis of an EM can usually be conveyed in a single sentence, or sometimes two. To express important expectations imbedded in an EM, a precis often assumes this form: When *x* occurs, *y* results.

Consider a memory from a young woman who recalled falling off a jungle gym as a girl.

EM 1. I was playing on the playground. I remember that I fell off the jungle gym, and I ran home. I got real embarrassed that I fell down in front of everyone, and I wouldn't go to the playground for the rest of the day. (What is clearest in the memory?) Falling down and everybody's looking at me. (What are you seeing in your mind's eye?) They weren't saying anything. They were just looking. I felt stupid. (What is the strongest feeling in the memory?) I just remembered that I wanted to get away from people. (You mean that you felt self-conscious and embarrassed?) Yeah.

The basic form of the EM can be summarized in the following precis, which focuses on perceptions, needs, interests, wishes, fears, expectations, major beliefs, and unresolved issues:

When I encounter difficulties with an achievement task, I feel embarrassed and self-conscious and [rather than continue to struggle] I withdraw [to avoid further risk of failing again].

The material in brackets is not explicitly stated but can be easily inferred from the memory. The major need (see Glossary of Needs) in the memory is achievement (trying to climb the monkey bars but failing). Her perception of herself in achievement contexts is inept and incompetent (she felt embarrassed and self-conscious). Her perception of others is critical and unsupportive (they stared). In terms of expectations, she appears primed to fail in achievement situations, suggesting in turn that she experiences considerable anxiety in such contexts. The EM therefore implies a strong fear of failure. Her major defenses when she feels inept and incompetent are to withdraw and avoid, which indicates that she will be extremely difficult to engage in treatment. Avoidant clients are difficult to help because they are afraid to take the risks that are necessary if they are to successfully resolve their problems. In extreme cases, they are afraid to initiate discussing their problems at all.

The meaning of precis should now be clear by example. Because we are interested in the form of the EM, the details are not important at this time. For instance, whether she fell from monkey bars or missed a word in a spelling bee is irrelevant in that the EM addresses the issue of mastery failure and her response tendency when confronted with same. Nor is it important to document in a precis whether there were three or thirty-three students watching her on the ground when she fell, whether it was a sunny or cloudy day, or whether she fell on asphalt or gravel. In sum, the precis attempts to uncover the form or structure which the details adorn—metaphorically speaking, the form of the tree (trunk, limbs) obscured by leaves. In most cases, the precis requires but a sentence or two.

Let us try another precis. Here is an early memory:

I remember getting a very bad spanking one time when my mother was dating my stepfather. They were going to the governor's inaugural ball, and I was so upset at my mother that they weren't taking me that I ripped the zipper out of her gown. (She laughs.) That wasn't very nice. (And is that how the memory ends?) Yes. (What is clearest in the memory?) I just remember crying a lot and screaming at my mother because she was going with my stepfather, who wasn't my stepfather at the time. (What is the strongest feeling at the time of the memory?) I think I felt guilty about doing it. I knew it was wrong.

The form of this memory is relatively simple, as witness the following precis: "I will do anything to get what I want, even when I know it is wrong."

But the client is not sociopathic in the classical sense. Her major need seems to be affiliation; she wants to be included and will absolutely not tolerate being excluded or separated from her primary attachment figure. Whereas the classic sociopath has turned away from people, this woman has relational problems. She desires closeness and is unwilling to tolerate any frustration of her need to be included and feel secure and valued.[1] She perceives herself as "not very nice" when these needs are frustrated, and feels "guilty" about how she acts but lacks the will to control herself from lashing out. In other words, she knows that she has a serious problem but is unwilling to compromise on her demands, which from her perspective are nonnegotiable. Her awareness and her guilt are not sufficient to restrain the expression of her rage or to cause her to modify her demands. In addition to impulse control problems around the expression of anger, there may also be deficits in communication skills (not knowing how to ask effectively for what she wants) although the EM is not clear on this point. In terms of expectations, she appears to expect to be excluded and rejected, which suggests perceived inadequacies about the self. In sum, the EM describes a vicious cycle in which she expects to be rejected by a significant other, provokes the other whom she believes will reject her anyway, and then is resoundingly rejected (e.g., "a very bad spanking"). Her expectations are thereby confirmed; moreover, her cycle of unreasonable demands, rejection, rageful retaliation, and guilt becomes further entrenched.

A third EM illustrates two common clinical problems of which the therapist should ideally be aware at the outset of treatment.

I remember playing under the back porch in the mud with my girlfriend. We were "playing house," mud being the food that we were mixing up, etc. Her mother came over—she was a very good friend of my mother—to tell my friend it was time to go home. I told my friend that if we were quiet her mother wouldn't notice us and would go up in the kitchen and chat with my mother, thus giving us more time to play. It happened that way, and when we were finally called, under much protest, Beverly had to go home.

The form of the memory is summarized by the following precis: "I will not ask for what I want because if I do, I expect that the request will be refused."

The major needs in this memory are a mix of achievement and affiliation needs, with the latter predominating. When the client must depend on someone else to cooperate, she is mistrustful. She perceives others as lacking in sensitivity to her needs, and she sees herself as lacking in personal clout (importance). Her expectation is that any direct statement of need will be rejected, so she has chosen instead to observe the habits and patterns of others and use this information to her advantage. In terms of defenses, we see a pattern of avoidance that has culminated in a problem with assertiveness and self-disclosure of needs. By adopting the role of the wily survivor, she learned how to meet her own needs successfully, thus bypassing a need for direct confrontation. When she was forced to petition others, she recalled that her requests were refused, thus reinforcing her expectations. It is interesting to note that this client presented in the same manner in treatment, disguising her true wishes and leaving me thoroughly confused as to her motive for seeking help. Once she made her EMs available, I said to her, "I see that you have had a life-long problem telling people what you want," which elicited a gasp of astonishment that her secret had been uncovered, and productive sessions thereafter.

IDENTIFYING MAJOR UNRESOLVED ISSUES IN EARLY MEMORIES

When we examine the form of the early memory, the unresolved issue or unfinished business can be identified either by inspection or inference. Let us return to the jungle gym memory for our first example. The form was: "When I encounter difficulties with an achievement task, I feel embarrassed and self-conscious and (rather than continue to struggle) I withdraw (to avoid further risk of failing again)."

Unresolved issues are most important in negative affect (fears) memories. We can ascertain whether an EM is negative by asking the client to rate the affect (see Bruhn, 1989, *EMP*, affect rating scales, pp. 9–10). The jungle gym memory is not only negative, it has a clear avoidant pattern: "When I encounter difficulties with an achievement task . . . I withdraw." By inspection, the form of the EM indicates that the client avoids achievement tasks which tells us there is an unresolved issue. It requires only a small inferential step to conclude that her problems with achievement are probably linked to her fear of failure and lack of self-confidence. Moreover, after reflecting upon her perceptions of others (they "stared"), we see that she does not expect to be supported and encouraged when she encounters difficulties, which will intensify her problems with mastery tasks. From this single EM the clinician not only has a reading on what is actually bringing the client into treatment, but he can also identify the proximate causes (at least) as well as what he can do to redress the problem. In this case, he needs to find some way to help the client reduce her level of anxiety, increase her self-confidence, and obtain additional support from teachers, peers, and family. What he does not know from the EM is what has historically caused her to fear failure and to perceive others as not supportive, something that the treatment process must elucidate.

Let us next try to identify the unfinished business in the ripped zipper memory. The form was: (general) "I will do anything to get what I want, even when I know it is wrong"; or (specific) "When I am excluded by significant others, I will ruin things for them and make them as miserable as I feel." This memory, like the jungle gym memory, is a negative affect memory, but it is not avoidant. The form reflects an acting out pattern rather than a withdrawing or avoidant response tendency. By inspection, the form of the memory indicates an inability to tolerate the frustration associated with not having her way (general), particularly when she wants to be included (specific). A small inferential step is needed to conclude that her unresolved issue involves using more socially appropriate methods (negotiation, compromise) to gratify her needs so that she will not be rejected by the very individuals who can gratify her social and affectional needs. The form of the memory suggests that she does not know what to do to help herself, likely because she expects to be excluded no matter what she does. If so, the therapist will need to do some teaching. Most important, he must help his client to accept that her interests will be better served if she tries to negotiate. The alternative is to continue to use power tactics that will almost inevitably cause her to be rejected. Such concepts are foreign to many acting-out individuals because their actions invariably gratify some needs (aggressive needs), and may, in addition, lead to the gratification of some demands early in the relationship. It is difficult to argue against a successful reinforcement schedule, which is the therapist's dilemma if his client is paired with a passive, approval-seeking, or conflict-avoidant significant other.

The back porch memory will provide the third illustration of an unresolved issue. The form was: "I will not ask for what I want because if I do, I expect the request will be refused." This memory, like the jungle gym memory, is a negative affect recollection, and the form is also avoidant. By inspection, the unresolved issues involve self-disclosure and

assertiveness. Note that when the major unresolved issue is self-disclosure, problems with assertiveness almost inevitably follow—that is, the
client who cannot disclose her needs usually will be unable to ask another
to gratify these needs (assert herself). Problems with self-disclosure also
lead to problems with intimacy, which requires that one disclose
thoughts, feelings, and needs.

The preceding memories illustrate three different unresolved issues:
overcoming a fear of failing associated with mastery tasks; finding an
appropriate means to gratify social and affectional needs and the need
to be included and valued; and being able to self-disclose and assert
oneself appropriately. As the preceding discussion suggests, many negative affect memories reveal not just the unresolved issue but also what
has caused the issue to become entrenched. The reader will discover
many different unresolved issues as familiarity is gained with applying
the Cognitive-Perceptual method to EMs; however, most will cluster
around a limited number of *meta-issues* involving *trust, separation/individ-
uation, cooperation, mastery, intimacy and understanding.*

EMs AS METAPHORS

Early memories frequently serve a metaphorical function by providing
a graphic visual picture of the client's difficulties. The metaphor usually
conveys the feeling tone associated with the problem as well.

Consider the following example of a man in his late thirties.

Background

A businessman with an almost legendary history of financial success
in the community came in for testing, complaining of depression. Considered a boy genius by his peers, he achieved exceptional success with
every project he touched. To the surprise of all who knew him, the client
purchased a company involved with a business that he had never dealt
with before. His reasoning was that adverse economic conditions had
caused the company to be discounted to bargain basement levels. Once
he took over operations, however, he discovered problems that far ex-
ceeded his most dismal scenario. Worse, he lacked the expertise to correct
the problems and worried that the sheer magnitude of the investment
might bring about his financial ruin.

His Early Memories

EM 1. They were building a building. There was a huge mound
of concrete. I thought it could support me, and it didn't. I went

up to my neck, and they pulled me out of it. (What is clearest in the memory?) I was sitting in my room all nice and dry and clean and looking out the window to the building where I was just plucked out of a problem. (What is the strongest feeling in the memory?) I don't remember the feeling, but it would probably be the helplessness I was feeling as I was in the concrete. I was probably four or five or six.

EM 2. I have more vivid memories after we moved from there. The most vivid memory was when I jumped into a bushel basket of glass. I didn't walk down the steps the right way, and I cut myself. I cut all the tendons in my left leg. (How did that happen?) I was barefooted. Somebody had broken glass, and my mom put it by the railing. Rather than walking down the steps, I leaped through the railing and ended up in the glass. (Sounds like you didn't expect to find the glass where it was?) Right. (What is clearest in the memory?) Being dashed over to the hospital.

Comment

The first EM suggests that he metaphorically feels up to his neck in trouble. The second EM warns, "Look before you leap." The relevance of these memories to his present difficulties is unmistakable. His impulsiveness and poor judgment brought him to the brink of financial ruin, just as the cement and the broken glass nearly caused his demise. An analysis of his living situation revealed a similar pattern in relation to his family. His impulsivity caused him to act in a parallel manner with insufficient forethought, thereby exposing him, and his family, to emotional distress.

It is my belief that these particular metaphorical memories were creatively selected by the client from his store of recollections to help him understand his own contribution to his current dilemma—a common function of autobiographical memory.

DWIGHT DAVID EISENHOWER: THE WARRIOR PRESIDENT

Thus far in this chapter, we have analyzed early memories from four individuals in a clinical population. What would EMs be like for particularly well-functioning individuals? Let us consider the first memory of President Dwight David Eisenhower.[2]

There are two primary benefits associated with analyzing the memories of well-known public figures. First, such individuals have left behind a public record that is germane to the interpretation of their memories.

This information is available to other professionals who may want to test the hypotheses that emerge from such analyses. Second, individuals who thrive despite the glare of public scrutiny are more likely to be successful and well-functioning. Their memories help us to understand some of the variables that contribute to success or, if you would prefer, an ability to function well under stress.

Eisenhower's memory will also provide an opportunity to introduce some new techniques, including the use of an afterthought in an EM.

Eisenhower: Background Information

Dwight D. Eisenhower (1890–1969) was Supreme Commander of the Allied Forces during World War II and the thirty-fourth president of the United States. Eisenhower's academic achievements and early military career were unremarkable. However, he later excelled in, and won recognition for, his ability to plan war games. His preparation of strategy for the Allied invasion of Europe during World War II and his ability to persuade and mediate earned him recognition that marked the beginning of a rapid advancement that culminated in his appointment to the position of Supreme Commander of the Allied Forces. As Supreme Commander, he brought about "the most dramatic, decisive event of the war" (Liddell Hart, 1967, p. 309), the massive invasion of France by Allied troops. The invasion began following Eisenhower's decision, after careful consideration, to attempt that undertaking in adverse weather conditions, a strategy that he considered risky but unlikely to pose a serious hazard. Military historians Dupuy and Dupuy (1970), in assessing Eisenhower's military career, report that he was an "excellent Allied soldier . . . who achieved such notable and deserved victories as to present to [his] people ideal images of the quintessence of charismatic military leadership" (p. 1,015).

A similar emphasis on displaying strength, backed by a well-publicized intent to use it if necessary, marked Eisenhower's career as president. Most notable in this regard was his decision, in response to increasing guerrilla warfare in Southeast Asia, Africa, and Cuba, to adopt a policy of "massive retaliation" as a deterrent to all kinds of aggression. On the home front, Eisenhower met the most important challenge of his incumbency by sending troops to Arkansas to end the governor's attempt to block school integration.

Eisenhower's Earliest Memory

What follows is a verbatim transcript of Eisenhower's earliest memory, as reported in his autobiography (1967).

My earliest memory involves an incident that occurred two or three months before my fifth birthday. I took a long trip to a strange and far-off place—Topeka—for a tough and prolonged war.

My sister's aunt, Aunt Minnie, was visiting us. We lived in a little cottage on Second Street in Abilene. It was decided that I would return with her to Topeka where a considerable number of Mother's relatives lived.

It was a day trip and during the course of the morning the heat of the railroad car and the monotony of the noise made me very sleepy. "Does this train have a sleeping car?" I asked her, using a scrap of worldly knowledge I had presumably picked up while listening to a family conversation. "It's not really necessary to go to a sleeping car," my aunt replied. "Just lie down on the seat and I'll make sure you have a good nap." I did and she was right.

After leaving the train, we next had to take a long ride by horse and buggy to my relatives' farm out beyond the northern outskirts of Topeka. I can remember looking down through the floorboards watching the ground rush past and the horses' feet, which seemed to slide. When we arrived, life became even more confusing. It was peculiar to be surrounded by so many strangers. It seemed to me that there were dozens or hundreds of people—all grownups—in the house. Even though they were, somehow, my family, I felt lonesome and lost among them.

I began to wander around outside. In the rear of the house was an old-fashioned well, very deep, with a wooden bucket and a long rope threaded through a pulley. My uncle Luther [*sic*] found me, fascinated by the well, and he offered a long story about what would happen to me if I fell in. He spoke in such horrible terms that I soon lost any ambition to look over the fearful edge into the abyss below. Looking around for less dreadful diversion, I noticed a pair of barnyard geese. The male resented my intrusion from our first meeting and each time thereafter he would push along toward me aggressively and with hideous hissing noises so threatening my security that five-year-old courage could not stand the strain. I would race for the back door of the house, burst into the kitchen, and tell any available elder about this awful old gander.

Thus the war began. In the early parts of the campaign, I lost a skirmish every half hour and invariably had to flee ignominiously and weeping from the battlefield. Without support, and lacking arms of any kind, it was only by recourse to distressing retreat after retreat to the kitchen door that I kept myself from disaster.

My enemy was that bad-tempered and aggressive gander. I was a little boy, not yet five years old, who was intensely curious about the new environment into which he was thrust and determined to explore its every corner. But the gander constantly balked me. He obviously looked upon me as a helpless and harmless nuisance. He had no intention of permitting anyone to penetrate his domain. Always hopeful that he would finally abandon his threatened attacks on my person, I'd try again and again, always with the same result.

Uncle Luther decided that something had to be done. He took a worn-out broom and cut off all the straw except for a short hard knob which he probably left so that in my zeal, if I developed any, I might not hurt my odd adversary. With the weapon all set, he took me out into the yard. He showed me how I was to swing and then announced that I was on my own.

The gander remained aggressive in his actions, and I was not at all sure that my uncle was very smart. More frightened at the moment of his possible scolding than I was of aggression, I took what was meant to be a firm, but was really a trembling, stand the next time the fowl came close. Then I let out a yell and rushed toward him, swinging the club as fast as I could. He turned and I gave him a satisfying smack right in the fanny. He let out a most satisfactory squawk and ran off. This was my signal to chase him, which I did.

From then on, he would continue his belligerent noises whenever he saw me (and the stick). He kept his distance and I was the proud boss of the back yard. I never make [*sic*] the mistake of being caught without the weapon. This all turned out to be a rather good lesson for me because I quickly learned never to negotiate with an adversary except from a position of strength. (pp. 29–30)

Traditional Interpretive Approaches

As discussed in Chapter 2, EMs can be interpreted from several perspectives. For example, Adlerians might stress Eisenhower's need to master obstacles and thereby overcome feelings of inferiority. The EM would also serve as a reminder that a difficult and often repeated struggle was finally won. From an ego-psychological perspective, the memory could be viewed as reflecting a whole period of development, the phallic, or phallic/Oedipal, condensed into a single event. Freudians might stress a pre-Oedipal, phallic narcissistic fixation that resulted from failures with Oedipal level issues. This perspective would stress a repetitive, almost compulsive need on Eisenhower's part to engage in phallic activities to prove himself as a man in light of previous failures that had occurred in these areas. These failures could be viewed as stimulating certain self-doubts and anxieties which Eisenhower compulsively defended himself against by returning again and again to battle until he was able, finally, to rout his enemy. A Freudian would likely argue that the earlier defeats and accompanying blows to his self-esteem appeared to activate self-doubts and a mistrust of others which strongly motivated Eisenhower to deal with others "from a position of strength."

The Cognitive-Perceptual Interpretation

Cognitive-Perceptual theory focuses on needs, interests, wishes, fears, expectations, major beliefs, unresolved issues and perceptions in early memories. The meta-issue in Eisenhower's memory involves mastery or achievement. This is likely a positive affect early memory, as opposed to a negative affect early memory (see, for example, the EMs from the clinical subjects). Therefore, in Eisenhower's memory we are looking more at a wish than a fear. The wish concerns mastery or achievement needs specifically related to competing successfully and maintaining control. As can be seen from Eisenhower's interactions with the gander, the memory divides into two parts much like a two-act play. In Act I, Eisenhower is routed repeatedly by the gander. In Act II, Eisenhower consults Uncle Luther, regroups his forces, and routs the gander. The memory deals with how he learned to function competently in a military-like arena and how he learned to overcome his fears in situations that required assertiveness. As has been noted, a logical place to begin the process of analysis is with a precis of the EM. "When I encounter difficulties in a competitive domain, I must seek counsel to find a means to overpower and defeat my opponent."

This memory shares some common elements with the jungle gym memory. Eisenhower is concerned with competing and winning. The jungle gym memory shadows Eisenhower's in the beginning, with both individuals withdrawing and retreating from a setback. The difference is that the young woman gives up whereas Eisenhower seeks guidance, returns to the fray, and achieves his goal.

In Eisenhower's EM the major issue is achieving mastery and control, accomplished by establishing dominance. At the end of the memory Eisenhower expresses the lessons that he extracted from his experience and applied to other adversarial situations. His concluding remarks bolster the hypothesis that this issue was a major, ongoing concern for him.

An examination of the major issue in the EM can also provide insight into the individual's needs and interests, as well as his perception of himself and others. Eisenhower's interests, as illustrated by his encounters with the gander, are predominantly competitive. He needs to be in control, to establish dominance when challenged, and to maintain a perception of himself as powerful and competent in dealing with the external world.

As Eisenhower perceives external reality, the world poses fearful and dangerous challenges. This perception is evident in his responses to the fearful abyss of the well; the security-threatening, horridly hissing gander; the long, disorienting trek to Topeka; and the confusing crowd of family he found once there. Eisenhower's initial perception of himself is one of weakness and inadequacy. This perception is evident in his need to separate himself from the overstimulation of being surrounded by a crowd of unfamiliar adults; in his apprehension about falling into the well if he did not find another activity with which to occupy himself; and in the discouragement which prompted him to seek counsel about how to deal with the gander.

Eisenhower's initial expectation is that help can be obtained from others when he is in need, and so there is a willingness to reach out. Consistent with this expectation, his description suggests that Uncle Luther was eventually perceived as both a wise and helpful care-giver and as an older role model with whom Eisenhower could identify. However, Luther did not infantilize him by rescuing him from a frightening but relatively harmless situation that might provide an occasion for learning and growth. It was not until Eisenhower suffered repeated defeats, complained to every available elder, and exhausted his own resources that Uncle Luther offered assistance. Even then, Eisenhower was left alone, though properly armed, to do battle with his adversary, the gander. Despite his doubts about Luther's advice, Eisenhower acted as instructed. His initial skepticism about his uncle's intelligence and judgment proved unfounded, thus strengthening the bond between himself and Luther as a role model. Eisenhower's success with the gander appears to have increased his self-confidence markedly. His perception of himself as weak and vulnerable was likewise altered, consistent with his revised expectation that he would prevail if properly prepared.

After the major issue in the EM has been identified, the affect should be analyzed, particularly any changes in affect that might occur with subsequent developments in the plot line. An examination of the affect may provide clues as to the reason that the major issue is important; changes in affect often correspond with alterations in schema as the lesson is assimilated. Further, the strength of the affect often provides an indication as to how emotionally laden the issue might be. In Eisenhower's EM, anxiety, self-doubt, and discouragement are the predominant initial affects. His account of his journey and subsequent visit suggests that at a deeper level Eisenhower is describing his reaction to being placed in novel situations, particularly those requiring a high level of mastery and control. His description of his feelings indicates that initially he felt confused as well as, perhaps, overwhelmed. However, the memory concludes on a note of triumphant pride. These affective changes encourage us to examine carefully the interplay between the affect and the major issue so as to better understand how the individual perceives the problem and his motivation for acting.

Eisenhower's preoccupation with mastery and control can be seen at several points in the EM: his use of "a scrap of worldly knowledge" in his talk with his aunt; his persistent engagement with the gander; and later, his comments about being armed and prepared for battle so that he might establish advantage. Yet, despite his extraordinary life achievements, there is nothing in the memory to suggest that Eisenhower responded to novelty or challenges with a ready reserve of self-confidence. Instead, we see an individual who struggled through the incident with a surprising burden of anxiety. His sense of triumph at the end of the memory provides some clues as to the agonizing tension which he likely experienced as he battled not just an external foe, but an internal one as well—his own self doubts and feelings of inadequacy. The intensity of both the initial and later affect provides a clue as to how important it was for Eisenhower to overcome obstacles and to boost his self-esteem via mastery activities.

Not permitting himself to become compromised by self-doubts, Eisenhower was determined to assert himself and explore his surroundings. His behavior suggested a belief that perserverance was necessary and that success, although expected, might be slow in coming. However, Eisenhower did not stubbornly persist with an inadequate strategy. Instead, when he encountered obstacles, he readily sought and accepted counsel from those who were wiser and more experienced. Having taken the advice of his uncle and triumphed over the gander, Eisenhower experienced pride and a sense of power. Eisenhower's style of confronting problems in a direct manner, of meeting strength with strength and winning, also gave him a sense of personal effectance and control (see Bruhn & Schiffman, 1982b).

Eisenhower's memory provides an excellent illustration of the interplay between the major issue and the affect in an EM. Analyzing how they interface often provides a clearer understanding of the individual and his behavior. For Eisenhower, the manifest issue is mastering his environment and demonstrating competence, but at a deeper level, his battles appear to afford a means for him to confront his anxieties and self-doubts and overcome them.

Since the memory is positive, there is no unresolved issue as such—Eisenhower emerged triumphant in his struggle with the gander. However, Eisenhower's comments emphasized the importance of being prepared and in control in the event of a confrontation: "I never make [*sic*] the mistake of being caught without the weapon. This all turned out to be a rather good lesson for me because I quickly learned never to negotiate with an adversary except from a position of strength" (p. 30). In sum, the memory functions as a warning about the importance of being prepared. In addition, the memory serves as a reminder both of the bitterness of defeat, as he was routed by the gander time and again, and of the triumph of victory—"I was the proud boss of the backyard."

Eisenhower's memory also provides an opportunity to introduce the concept of an *afterthought*. From the broadest perspective, autobiographical memories function as a personal storehouse of knowledge. They play out in concrete terms what we have learned about ourselves, others, the world, and life in general. The afterthought, when it appears in a memory, usually occurs at the very end. It contains the individual's epilogue, or his most significant thoughts or conclusions about the matter in question. Afterthoughts are relatively rare in autobiographical memories. When they occur, they indicate that the individual has spent extra time pondering and reflecting upon the broader meaning of the event. They underscore the importance of the memories in which they appear, particularly their ongoing contemporary relevance. In Eisenhower's case, the memory reminds him to be vigilant, to be prepared, and to be on guard. Afterthoughts will also be discussed in the next section on Golda Meir's EMs.

The circumstances of Eisenhower's life are a matter of public record. For much of his adult life, Eisenhower occupied positions of power and authority in military and political arenas. His judicious choice of, and reliance on, close advisors was apparent, as was his insistence on demonstrating strength in adversarial situations, all of which is consistent with the image of the man depicted in the memory. In his recollection the gander was smacked once in the backside and chased. Eisenhower sought respect from his opponents. If provoked, he retaliated, but only to the extent of establishing dominance—as occurred when he sent troops to Arkansas to ensure school desegregation. As president, Eisenhower appointed excellent cabinet officers, soliciting and following advice which made sense to him, much as he did with his Uncle Luther. Nor is it surprising in hindsight that we see Eisenhower in his recollection on the receiving end of orders, for a good general must first be a good soldier.

Summary

The earliest memory of Dwight David Eisenhower was analyzed to illustrate the use of the Cognitive-Perceptual method and what can be learned about Eisenhower. A precis was undertaken, and the major issue raised in the memory was identified and linked with the dominant affect. The affect provides another means to assess the individual's status with his major issue. Attitudes and perceptions, for instance, tend to be mood consistent. The strength of the affect also provides another means to gauge the importance of major issue. Changes in the plot line which alter the quality or magnitude of the affect are noteworthy as they call attention to coping devices, or their absence, which the individual has employed to help him resolve the major issue. These coping devices function to minimize the emotional impact of the unresolved problem.

Eisenhower's recollection of his repeated but initially futile attempts to avoid defeat reflects his need to attain a goal that was blocked. His repeated failures and his frequent pleas for help point to the enormous internal tension he experienced to complete the action line of the memory and attain his goal. His memory graphically illustrates how an unresolved issue can profoundly alter one's self-perception. Only when the major issue is resolved will the associated affect dissipate and the perception of self and others shift. Eisenhower's EM reflects a partial working through of feelings of inadequacy associated with competitive and aggressive situations. The memory vividly illustrates how he is likely to respond when he is provoked and challenged by others who attempt to dominate him.

THE EARLIEST MEMORIES OF GOLDA MEIR

All of us have experienced traumas, failures, losses, and frights in our lifetime. If so, does this mean that the course of our lives has been forever determined by such experiences? Although some may experience such events in an extreme form, or in greater number, in the final analysis the question is what does the individual make of such experiences? Some doubt themselves, others withdraw from the world, whereas others become more cautious about taking chances. By contrast, some individuals become more determined, and such experiences harden their resolve to reach their goal. Traumas, then, need not break an individual; instead they may create a stronger sense of purpose and direction. When such events are recalled as EMs, they function as a basic roadmap for keeping the individual centered on a significant life goal while at the same time disclosing his motivation for achieving the goal.[3]

What is the relationship, then, between content themes in EMs and present attitudes and concerns? Consider victimization memories. Attitudes and associated affects imbued in the spontaneous recollections of past events similarly exist in present time. In fact, present mood and attitudes determine what is recalled from the past. With but rare exceptions, only what is mood consistent and consonant with present attitudes will be recalled from one's early past as spontaneous EMs. Thus, the individual who recalls being victimized in the past is angry in the present. In fact, it is present anger and present feelings of alienation that are expressed in the content of being victimized in the past. The thematic material provides expression for the affect and reveals its roots.

Data to support this line of reasoning comes from a number of sources: Bartlett (1932) argued from his research that memory function conforms to and reflects present attitudes; Bach (1952) and Mosak (1958, 1969) pointed out that when clients' attitudes and beliefs change during the course of psychotherapy their EMs are likewise altered, or changed entirely, to reflect their new beliefs; similarly, regarding recent memories and associated attitude changes, Neisser (1982) cited a Goethals and Reckman (1973) study that demonstrates, as Neisser puts it, "people often cannot remember what they used to believe" (p. 178). In addition, it is further proposed that the feelings and attitudes depicted in EMs may be dealt with in present time in a manner that may be pathological or adaptive. How such feelings are dealt with becomes a significant consideration in assessing pathology because similar situations today are likely to elicit the same response tendencies and the same coping mechanisms.

Early Memories and Afterthoughts

If an individual can detach herself from the major issue in her EM and regard it with a sense of perspective, she often has the capability to deal adaptively with her feelings in the memory. Making this determination helps us to assess coping skills as well as the type and extent of pathology. One step in this assessment is to analyze the afterthought in a memory, which typically consists of the following: a concluding remark regarding what the experience meant to the individual, how it affected her, and how she made use of the experience subsequently. However, afterthoughts are infrequent. The inclusion of an afterthought suggests an ability to reflect about past experience, to extract lessons from that experience, and to make conscious use of these lessons in the present. Although many well-functioning individuals append afterthoughts to their EMs, in my experience, most individuals from a clinical population do not. Those clients who include afterthoughts will typically draw irrational, pathological conclusions from their experience—for example, "after that, I learned not to trust teachers"; "I found out that people were out for all they can get so you shouldn't trust nobody." More commonly, clients will remark, when asked what a memory meant to them, "It was just something that happened," or "I don't know why it sticks with me, it's just a memory that I have." Although the feelings and attitudes that appear in the memory mirror the client's present responses to people and situations, that connection is rarely made. Less frequently, as in the case of Golda Meir, former Prime Minister of Israel, the individual has pondered the relationship between present and past and can make those connections. The EMs that follow are all taken from Meir's autobiography, *My Life* (1975).

Golda Meir's Earliest Memory

In a way, I suppose that the little I recall of my early childhood in Russia, my first eight years, sums up my beginnings, what now are called the formative years. If so, it is sad that I have very few happy or even pleasant memories of this time. The isolated episodes that have stayed with me throughout the past seventy years have to do mostly with the terrible hardships my family suffered, with poverty, cold, hunger and fear, and I suppose my recollection of being frightened is the clearest of all memories. I must have been very young, maybe only three and a half or four. We lived then on the first floor of a small house in Kiev, and I can still recall distinctly hearing about a pogrom that was to descend on us. I didn't know then, of course, what a pogrom was, but I knew it had something to do with being Jewish and with the rabble that used to surge through town, brandishing knives and huge sticks, screaming "Christ killers" as they looked for the Jews, and who were now going to do terrible things to me and to my family.

I can remember how I stood on the stairs that led to the second floor, where another Jewish family lived, holding hands with their little daughter and watching our fathers trying to barricade the entrance with boards of wood. That pogrom never materialized, but to this day I remember how scared I was and how angry that all my father could do to protect me was to nail a few planks together while we waited for the hooligans to come. And, above all, I remember being aware that this was happening to me because I was Jewish, which made me different than most of the other children in the yard. It was a feeling that I was to know again many times during my life—the fear, the frustration, the consciousness of being different and the profound instinctive belief that if one wanted to survive, one had to take effective action about it personally. (pp. 13–14)

The precis in this case is, "As a Jew, one expects to be persecuted and attacked by non-Jews."

Next, Meir's perceptions of self, others, and world will be assessed. The major issue must also be identified as well as its interplay with the stronger affective elements in the memory.

In Meir's first memory—her "clearest"—we find a perception of self as vulnerable, a perception of significant others, especially father, as ineffectual in providing care and protection, and a perception of the environment as hostile, dangerous and anti-Semitic. In this memory we do not find the kind of victimization reported (Bruhn & Davidow, 1983; Davidow & Bruhn, 1990) in the memories of delinquents; here no physical harm occurs. However, the threat of victimization permeates the memory. Consistent with the preceding analysis, we find that the dominant affect in the memory is not anger but fright—note that Meir finds her "recollection of being frightened is the clearest of all my memories" (p. 13). Negative affect (fear) dominates this recollection, rather than events. When affect in an EM is the focal point, it has been my experience that well-adjusted individuals have learned to cope with such affects adaptively. By contrast, individuals seen clinically either have been unable to find ways to keep such feeling states to a tolerable level or they act in a self-destructive manner that creates the very feelings they wish to avoid. In Meir's case we will assume, due to the strength of the affect, that considerable energy is devoted to minimizing her fears and keeping them in check. The major issue for her, then, is to satisfy her security needs.

How can we assess Meir's coping skills from her first memory? From one viewpoint, we cannot. The memory poses the problem, but it does not reveal the solution. Eisenhower's first memory, by contrast, is clearly a mastery memory. After being repeatedly attacked and routed by a hostile gander, Eisenhower was taught by his Uncle Luther how to defend himself by counterattacking effectively. He stated that he learned from the experience "never to negotiate with an adversary except from a position of strength," an example of an afterthought. In Meir's case, we find a comparable assimilation of past experience: "If one wanted to survive, one had to take effective action about it personally" (p. 14). In both memories we find excellent examples of afterthoughts. Although we do not see a specific resolution to the problem posed in Meir's memory, she accepted it as her responsibility to resolve. We are also left with the unmistakable impression that she—unlike Eisenhower—relied on herself and kept her own counsel, for in her memory she perceived the attempts by the fathers to defend her and the community as totally inadequate.

Meir's subsequent EMs permit us to test our initial hypotheses for consistency. Often, but not always, the first early memory provides the key to understanding how the individual perceives and organizes her phenomenological world; accordingly, it deserves special attention. Further, the first memory is often recalled first due to reasons of primacy—that is, the issue raised in the memory has greatest importance for the individual. Meir's subsequent memories can be examined with the preceding in mind.

In her second memory, the affective tone shifts from fear to frustration and anger over perceived injustices.

Meir's Second Early Memory

Also, I remember all too clearly how poor we were. There was never enough of anything, not food, not warm clothing, not heat at home. I was always a little too cold outside and a little too empty inside. Even now, from that very distant past, I can summon up with no effort at all, almost intact, the picture of myself sitting in tears in the kitchen, watching my mother feed some of the gruel that rightfully belonged to me to my sister, Zipke. Gruel was a great luxury in our home in those days, and I bitterly resented having to share any of it, even with the baby. Years later I was to experience the dread of my own children's hunger and to learn for myself what it was like to have to decide which child was to receive more food, but, of course, in that kitchen in Kiev, I knew only that life was hard and there was no justice anywhere. (p. 14)

Precis: "What was rightfully mine was given to another."

Dramatically, the memory focuses on feelings of deprivation combined with injustice. Meir does not simply recall lacking a sufficiency of what she needs, which would suggest feelings of deprivation associated with depression, but she recalls someone getting what is rightfully hers. The issue in this memory, then, involves a struggle with resentment, apparently a long-term problem, as suggested by her comment, "Years later, I was to experience the dread of my own children's hunger and to learn for myself what it was like to have to decide which child was to receive more food . . . " (p. 14). Just as Eisenhower recalled being able, after many defeats, to assert himself against the gander, Meir's comment also suggests that she was finally able to resolve this issue for herself, at least to some extent. In her case, she was able to empathize with her mother's anguish when she herself became a mother and was forced to make the same unhappy choice of deciding which of her own children would eat.

What relation does Meir's first memory have to her second? At first glance, the two memories appear to have little in common. Even the dominant affects seem to differ. On closer inspection, however, Meir plays the role of helpless "victim" in her second memory, a role that she detests and ultimately rejects, as indicated in her closing comment to her first memory. Actually, Meir is not "victimized" in the sense that someone *does* something to her; rather, she is not adequately protected in the first memory and inadequately nurtured in the second. The message to the self in the second memory is, "I need and deserve more than I get," a narcissistic statement of importance and entitlement. Retrospectively, it is apparent that the same self message applies to her first memory. Moreover, a key affect emerges in both—her "dread" of her children's hunger in EM 2 resonates with the fear she felt in her first memory. Once the commonality in affects—fear and dread—is apparent in the memories, the commonalities in the issues also become obvious.

Family Myths as Early Memories

Bruhn and Bellow (1987) reported a variant of early memory that had not been discussed previously in the literature. This type of recollection is not, strictly speaking, an EM because it is not an event that the individual recalls as having happened to him once; however, it does provide a broader context for a set of EMs to be viewed and analyzed. The function of this memory is to preserve a family myth. Typically, the memory itself is highly overworked, so that details are either lost entirely or highly stylized as if they were selected or "created" with the message of the memory in mind. These memories are told and retold in the family over the years, with the intent, overt or covert, to preserve certain lessons, particularly for the younger generation. These memories are analogous in purpose to tribal folklore that preserves vital information for the tribal group so as to guide and direct it and keep it centered on its historical course. Many biblical "stories" serve a similar function for the Judeo-Christian community. Meir's next memory appears to be of this type—a family myth.

> My parents were newcomers in Kiev. They had met and married in Pinsk, where my mother's family lived, and it was to Pinsk that we all returned within a few years—in 1903, when I was 5. My mother was very proud of her romance with my father and told us about it often, but although I came to know the story by heart, I never tired of hearing it. My parents had been married very unconventionally, without benefit of a *shadchan*, the traditional matchmaker. (p. 14)

What is the focal point of this family myth? The major message is that women in Meir's family of origin are valued for their independence and self-sufficiency. They are expected to take charge of their lives, rather than rely on matchmakers or, by extension, on fathers and husbands to make important life decisions for them. The memory also has an iconoclastic, rebellious quality about it in the context of its romantic idealism. Meir's mother is not merely independent, she violates well-established social precepts to achieve her aim. Meir's account suggests a defiant pride associated with this way of acting, as if Meir were saying, "See, I don't need you, I can do this by myself." Thus, it appears that Meir, and her family, respect strong, independent women, women who can think for themselves. As we reflect back to her first EM, this family myth seems to provide the "go-ahead" she needs to assume the role of "family protector," traditionally a male role, by permitting her to act independently.

When we compare Meir's view of her mother to that of her father, the contrast so far is striking—a strong mother and a weak, largely ineffectual father. Thus, it might appear that she idealizes her mother and disdains her father for his weakness. However, as the following memory illustrates, this hypothesis is incorrect.

> But my mother had other troubles. Four little boys and a girl all fell ill: Two of them died before they were a year old, two of them went within one month. My mother mourned each of her babies with a broken heart, but like most Jewish mothers of that generation, she accepted the will of God and drew no conclusions about child rearing from the row of little graves. Then, right after the last of the babies had died, a well-to-do family who lived near us offered my mother a job as wet nurse to their new baby. They made one condition: My parents and Sheyna were to move from their miserable damp little room to a larger, lighter, airier one and a nurse was to come teach my poor young mother the rudiments of child care. So it was thanks to this single "foster child" that Sheyna's life improved and that I was born into relative order, cleanliness and health. (pp. 16–17)

This memory underscores one aspect of our preceding impression of Meir—that she values competence, which, for her, assumes—literally—life and death importance. Of course, luck also plays a role, through the largesse of the wealthy family. But although luck is necessary, it is not sufficient to guarantee survival.

Do other family myths support these hypotheses? The next focuses on her grandfather Mabovitch, a man who died long before she was born but whose influence remained years after his passing in the lessons that were extracted from his life.

> I don't know to what extent any of my grandparents influenced me, although in Pinsk I lived with my mother's parents for a long time. Certainly it is hard for me to believe that my father's father played any role at all in my life, since he died before my parents met. But somehow or other he became one of the personalities that people my childhood, and now, going back into the past, I feel he belongs to this story. He had been one of the thousands of "kidnapped" Jewish children of Russia, *shanghaied* into the Czar's army to serve for twenty-five years. Ill-clothed, ill-fed, terrified children, more often than not they were under constant pressure to convert to Christianity. My Mabovitch grandfather had been snatched by the Army when he was all of 13, the son of a highly religious family, brought up to observe the finest points of Orthodox Jewish tradition. He served in the Russian army another thirteen years, and never once, despite threats, derision and often punishment, did he

touch *treife* [non-kosher] food. All of those years he kept himself alive on uncooked vegetables and bread. Though pressed hard to change his religion and often made to pay for his refusal by being forced to kneel for hours on a stone floor, he never gave in. (pp. 17–18)

The message in this family myth is strikingly similar to her initial portrait of her mother. Grandfather is portrayed as independent, tough, resolute, and tenacious; he steadfastly holds to his religious convictions despite harassment from the majority Christian community in Russia. The message of this myth is the importance of maintaining one's integrity as a Jew. Grandfather Mabovitch thus functions as an ideal for Meir: "Do not capitulate to the forces of oppression. Stand up for your convictions and do not give in." This aspect of Mabovitch's life thus serves as an inspiration for Meir and contrasts with her father's actions in her first memory. We also find embedded in this story a basic premise of the Zionist movement that Meir was to influence—alone, only the most courageous, determined, and lucky survive. True security and religious freedom can be achieved only through the actions of Jews as a united community, an inference that follows from the "unfinished business" in her first memory.

Group Memories

Early memories may reflect attitudes associated with one or more group identifications. Groups can be defined along gender, ethnic, social class, regional, racial, or religious lines, to name several of the more likely possibilities. That an individual has made a strong group identification cannot be assumed simply because he or she is nominally qualified to be a member. Early memories often provide evidence that a group identification has taken place.

Group memories typically reflect the belief that the individual is "special" or "different" in some way. Her differentness may be viewed as having good or bad consequences, depending on how she had come to view the group that she has identified with. For instance, I have observed that many blacks in this country so identify themselves in their EMs and view their blackness as having aversive consequences. In their EMs, many blacks recall discrimination and prejudice associated with their discovery of themselves as black. For them, being black means unfair, arbitrary treatment—a type of victimization. However, recollections of victimization associated with a group identification differ from recollections of victimization found in the EMs of acting out individuals—for example, delinquents (Bruhn & Davidow, 1983; Davidow & Bruhn, 1990). Delinquents recall someone doing something to them as individuals, whereas in a group memory the individual constructs the action as being directed toward a target group. An example of the latter is a black college student who recalled wanting to go swimming in a municipal pool only to be told by her grandmother that she could not because the pool was for "whites only." A group victimization memory imprints in the individual's awareness that she should expect poor treatment from individuals who are not members of her group. In such memories, anger and hurt are associated with being victimized, but the anger is directed primarily toward non-group members who victimize rather than expressed as a generalized antisocial reaction.

Meir's EMs reflect a Jewish group identification. In her case Russian Christians were initially responsible for the prejudice and persecution she experienced. Her first memory reflects her Jewish identification as she suffers through the terror of a pogrom. One might guess that Zionists—a subgroup of Jews who strongly identify with the state of Israel—would tend to have memories that are psychologically similar to Meir's. One crucial element in Meir's attitude toward her Jewishness was her belief that she must take personal responsibility for her own survival. It is hypothesized that the EMs of other strongly self-identified Zionists will contain similar attitudes.

Discussion

Meir's EMs and family myths indicate that her major issue concerns security needs. It was pointed out that the first memory is often first for reasons of primacy, and Meir's first memory graphically depicts her need for security. The afterthought in her first early memory expresses her belief that she must assume personal responsibility for her own security and not look to others, particularly males, for help and protection. Various stories from her family—what have been termed family myths—provide insight into how she believed she must be in order to satisfy her security needs. Like her mother, she must be independent and willing to break with traditional ways of doing things in order to succeed. Unlike her mother in her younger years, she must be knowledgeable and competent. Like Grandfather Mabovitch, she must be tough, tenacious, resolute, and always faithful to her Jewish roots. The apparent contradiction between Meir as a traditionalist and as an iconoclast is resolved by her emphasis on taking personal responsibility for her own security needs. In the final analysis she believed that she must do whatever she had to do to achieve her aims and survive but still remain true to her identity as a Jew.

Fortunately, her autobiography, which provided us with her EMs, also provides information about her life as a whole so that the preceding hypotheses can be tested. Other sources will provide supplementary information.

Let us begin with Meir's own comment (Moritz et al., 1970) about the effect of the pogrom that she recalled as her first EM: "If there is any logical explanation . . . for the direction my life has taken . . . [it is] the desire and determination to save Jewish children . . . from a similar experience" (p. 284). In her autobiography, she states with regard to some of her anxieties as prime minister, "The real problems, as they had been for so long, were survival and peace, in that order" (p. 386). Earlier, she remarked, with a finely honed sense of irony, that Israelis "weren't interested in a fine, liberal, antimilitaristic, DEAD Jewish state . . . or in a settlement that would win us compliments . . . but that would endanger our lives" (p. 373). Other statements suggest that Israel was for her an extension of herself as a child as she suffered through the terror of the pogrom: "Jews neither can nor should ever depend on anyone else for permission to stay alive" (p. 159). That she not only believed in personal responsibility, as she stated in her first EM, but also made this a central axiom in her personal and political life is reflected in her reaction to her friend Haile Selassie's failure to stand by Israel: "It proved to me once again—although I didn't need very much more proof by then—one can count on no one but one's self" (p. 341).

Meir admired her mother's independence but mistrusted her weakness. As the "mother of Israel" she protected her "child" with the ferocity of a lioness protecting her cub. She would never again sit back and allow herself or her country to be victimized. She emphasized the need for self-protection because to her sorrow, as she put it, "There are still people who do not understand that we are committed to live and act so that those Jews who were killed in the gas chambers will have been the last Jews ever to have died without defending themselves" (p. 180). Yet, perhaps because she understood too well the meaning of human suffering, taking the initiative did not mean engaging in "wanton violence" (p. 189) but rather repelling a specific attack. Indeed, she was "unalterably opposed . . . to terror of any kind" (p. 196), an understandable position considering her first EM. However, when attacked, Meir responded with a terrifying retaliatory blow. For example, she approved the escalation of Israeli military action following increased terrorist attacks on Israeli targets in 1972, saying "Crush the heads of the terrorist Hydra" (Derogy & Carmel, 1979, p. 232). Similarly, Meir agreed to a plan to form killer-commando groups following the 1972 attack on the Israeli Olympic team in Munich. And she approved a plan effecting a decision to lure Soviet planes into a trap and fire upon them after learning of their presence in the region during the 1970 Israeli-Egyptian war (see Derogy & Carmel, 1979, p. 249). The deaths of six Israeli citizens by Jordanians, according to Neff (1981), led to her approval of a general policy of massive retaliatory attacks against Jordan in 1957. It was in this manner that Meir pursued her government's foreign policy. Ben-Gurion described her as "the strongest man in the cabinet" (The Insight Team of the *London Sunday Times*, 1974, p. 388), while Steven (1980) viewed her as being "as tough a politician as Israel ever had" (p. 205). Her "track record," both in and out of office "suggested a flinty attitude to any idea that might compromise Israel's security" (p. 388). They also noted Meir's realization that "to achieve anything, her country would have to seize the initiative while it could" (p. 388) or face, as Meir (1975) put it, "being killed off, either piecemeal or in one sudden attack" (p. 296).

It appears that Meir's basic approach to her problems was adaptive rather than pathological. Nevertheless, her perception of the world as threatening and hostile, of herself as a potential victim, and of others as ineffectual in assisting and protecting her are not unlike the perceptions of a delinquent (Bruhn & Davidow, 1983; Davidow & Bruhn, 1990). Indeed, such perceptions often lead either to acting out, antisocial behavior or to an anxious, paranoid state. In Meir's case, however, the dangers were real. The question was whether Meir would respond pathologically or adaptively to these dangers. Meir's EMs suggest that she could mobilize the strength and resources that she needed to cope with these dangers. She responded to her feelings of outrage by taking personal responsibility and attempting to defend the weak and vulnerable, thereby affording herself and her nation greater security. Her response was adaptive in that it helped reduce the level of fear that she so eloquently expressed in her earliest EM.

It has been argued in this section that the past can be used either adaptively or pathologically, depending on how events are constructed and understood. Meir herself often used her past experiences in a conscious way. She actively recalled childhood experiences and used these recollections to motivate herself to avoid re-experiencing the misery and terror of her past. Meir described her sister as reminding her to "never forget who you are" (p. 243). Meir took this advice seriously, even to the point of confronting Pope Paul VI during an audience when he criticized what he considered was harsh Israeli policy. She told him acidly, "Your holiness, do you know what my own very earliest memory is? It is waiting for a pogrom in Kiev. Let me assure you that we learned about real mercy when we were being led to the gas chambers by the Nazis" (p. 408).

Whether or not an individual consciously uses his EMs to guide his life as Meir did, EMs contain the essence of what has been distilled from important life experiences as well as the central issue that occupies his attention now.

LEE IACOCCA'S FAMILY PATTERN MYTHS

Family myths can be divided into two broad types: (1) a family member's story about an event that occurred when the individual was not present (e.g., Golda Meir's); (2) pattern memories (recollections of events that occurred more than once) that editorialize about the meaning of life and its conduct, express opinions about what one can expect from others, and the like. Such messages typically come from members of the nuclear or extended family. Pattern myths usually contain highly distilled abstract statements that function as axioms. Such axioms exert an enormous organizing influence on the personality. Pattern myths reveal a filtering and interpreting process that mirrors the operation of the belief system. The same filtering process is likely to operate with other family members. This is one reason that family members tend to think in similar ways and validate each other's experience.

From a clinical perspective, the therapist must identify the family's axioms and understand their implications, else little meaningful communication can take place. Once a major axiom changes, however, important family changes often follow.

Examples of family myths frequently appear in the autobiographies of public figures. Such individuals often want to share with others their recipe for success or their vision of the world—evident in Lee Iacocca's (1984) autobiography—or they attempt to use the autobiography as a podium to explain key actions in their lives. The latter is evident in Golda Meir's (1975) autobiography, as we have just seen.

Iacocca's book provides some clear examples of family myths of the pattern type. For instance, on the first page of chapter 1, Iacocca states: "For Nicola and Antoinette [his parents], America was the land of freedom—the freedom to become anything you wanted to be, if you wanted it bad enough and were willing to work for it. That was the single lesson my father gave to his family. I hope I have done as well with my own" (p. 3). His internalization of this lesson is evident throughout the book. For instance, he states in its introduction: "I learned that the real spirit of America is a kind of pragmatic optimism: Everything will turn out well in the end, but only if you struggle and sacrifice to make it happen" (p. x). As his statements indicate, Iacocca gained an enduring feeling of optimism from this axiom. He believed that he could control significant events in his life and that with hard work and persistence he could accomplish almost anything. Much of the rest of the book proves the truth of these axiomatic statements from his perspective. When he was fired by Henry Ford, he remembered what his father told him, and these thoughts sustained him when he became so discouraged that he developed an excessive reliance on alcohol. For Iacocca, things would work out if he put enough hard work into making things work out. The outcome was his to determine. His schematic perception of the world (America) was that it was an open, inviting place where outcomes were determined solely by one's actions.

Once assimilated into the personality organization such axioms become internal regulators of derived attitudes. For example: you are responsible for the kind and quality of the life you live; if you do not like what is happening now, do something about it; you can overcome the potentially crippling effects of ethnic and racial prejudice if you are willing to work hard enough. Each is a specific derivative of Iacocca's original axiom.

In the case of a well-functioning individual whose behavior derives from a small corpus of major axioms, a change in one such axiom can cause profound changes in mood and personality. In Iacocca's case, consider the impact of a hypothetical repudiation of his father's lesson that "most significant events in our lives are beyond our control." Similarly, "If luck is not on your side, there is little you can do." An acceptance of these axioms would cause major behavioral and mood changes under conditions of adversity or failure.

LATER MEMORIES, AFTERTHOUGHTS, AND GANDHI

Sometimes memories of later events can clarify conflict areas in a dramatic fashion. After a sample of early memories has been obtained, the writer uses the following probe: "Do you have any other memories that are particularly clear or important for any reason?" (see also the sixth memory in the Early Memories Procedure). This probe generally taps an important later memory.

Mahatma Gandhi (Fischer, 1962) recounted a later memory that exerted an important influence in his life. Gandhi, who lived from 1869 to 1948, was a young twenty-three-year-old attorney when he landed in Durban, Natal, in 1893 en route to Pretoria, South Africa. Gandhi had been engaged to come to South Africa to file a lawsuit on behalf of his client. Having taken first class accommodations at Durban, Gandhi was discovered by a white man in Maritzburg the next morning and forcibly extruded by a police constable when he refused to leave voluntarily. Banished to the cold of the winter, Gandhi remembered:

My overcoat was in my luggage but I did not dare to ask for it . . . lest I might be insulted and assaulted once again. I sat and shivered. . . .

Sleep was out of the question. . . .

I began to think of my duty. Should I fight for my rights or go back to India or should I go on to Pretoria without minding the insults and return to India after finishing the case? It would be cowardice to run back to India without fulfilling my obligation. The hardship to which I was subjected was superficial—only a symptom of the deep disease of color prejudice. I should try, if possible, to root out the disease and suffer hardships in the process. Redress for wrongs I should seek only to the extent that would be necessary for the removal of the color prejudice.

This resolution somewhat pacified and strengthened me but I did not get any sleep.

I suffered further insults and received more beatings on my way to Pretoria. But all this only confirmed me in my determination.

Thus . . . I obtained full experience of the condition of Indians in South Africa. (pp. 36–37)

Years later, Gandhi was asked to name the most "creative experience" in his life (Fischer, 1962). In reply, Gandhi recounted his memory of the preceding event. To feel victimized, impotent, and angry would not be unusual under the circumstances. However, Gandhi rose above those feelings, seeking instead to educate those who oppressed him and his people. He decided to eliminate the cause of the problem or what he referred to as the "disease"—"color prejudice." The afterthought in Gandhi's memory is essential. Without it, we would miss the major issue in the memory—understanding. Gandhi believed that he must experience before he could truly understand. He processed the injustices that he suffered as experiences which increased his understanding and thereby fueled his determination.

HISTORICAL CAUSALITY, THE RECOLLECTIONS OF SPECIFIC EVENTS, AND BILL BRADLEY

Many clinicians believe that EMs either reflect traumas or function as screens for traumas that have had a deterministic influence on personality development. Regarding historical causality, CP theory holds that most EMs simply reflect present-day attitudes that the individual associates to a particular incident in the past. In actuality, these may or may not have caused him to believe as he does now.

In many cases, it is not the event that caused the person to develop along particular lines but the nature of the personality itself. The recollected event merely provides a catalyst for various aspects of the personality, which are already in place, to merge and solidify. A memory from Bill Bradley, a former NBA star for the New York Knickerbockers, U.S. senator from New Jersey, and a frequently mentioned Democratic candidate for president, illustrates the point. The memory was reported by David Halberstam (1988):

Certainly, his [Bradley's] parents sent subliminal messages of their own that he, their only child, should amount to something. There was no lack of ambition in the family. His mother wanted him to be a success; his father wanted him to be a gentleman. "I was," he notes somewhat laconically, "raised to be a successful gentleman." There was always a remarkable willingness to work, to pay the price of his own ambition. He tells how, at 15, he went to the summer basketball camp run by Easy Ed Macauley, a former college and pro star. "Just remember that if you're not working at your game to the utmost of your ability," Macauley told his assembled campers, "there will be someone out there somewhere with equal ability who will be working to the utmost of his ability. And one day you'll play each other, and he'll have the advantage." There seemed to Bradley to be a totality of truth in those words. Some 30 years later, he not only remembers that moment but also notes: "The important thing about the story is the type of young man I was, who would be so totally accepting of words like that and who, hearing them, immediately acted on them." (p. 5)

In Bradley's case it is apparent that he was primed to hear Macauley's message. Opportunity converged with readiness. Cognitive-Perceptual theory holds that Bradley's memory is not an isolated instance of this phenomenon. We recall, for the most part, what we have been prepared to believe. Whether the belief mirrored by the memory is directly attributable to the event in question, whether it is a product of many experiences that have occurred over a lifetime, or whether it reflects more recent experiences is an open question. However, Cognitive-Perceptual theory holds that, with rare exceptions, EMs reflect present beliefs, no matter what the historical source of causality, and that the event in question is recalled first and foremost consistent with the principle of attraction.

PROCESS INTERPRETATIONS OF EARLY MEMORIES

A series of EMs may be conceptualized in this manner.[4] The earliest memory is typically determined by the major issue having greatest priority. This memory emerges in conformance with the principle of attraction to best express the major issue. The historical realities originally associated with this event are creatively revised to give appropriate expression to this issue. In extreme cases, the memory may be completely fabricated—e.g., such as the ripped zipper memory reported earlier in this chapter. Subsequent EMs typically clarify and elaborate the major issue and provide information as to how the individual typically copes with this problem. While every set of EMs does not conform to this pattern, it is by far the most common.

Let us consider an illustration of what we see when the major issue involves separation/individuation. The earliest memory typically presents the major issue, which is derived from the precis (e.g., "I become anxious and insecure when those who are close to me leave"). The second and subsequent EMs commonly elaborate the major theme found in the precis (e.g., "When I feel special in a relationship, I feel more comfortable") and provides information as to how the individual attempts to cope (e.g., by withdrawing).

Process interpretation is concerned with two matters—identifying the major issue and understanding how that issue is handled as the set of spontaneous EMs unfolds.

The major issue, as has been discussed, can be determined from the precis. The task of identifying the major issue changes somewhat when the clinician works with a set of EMs in that a set of precis interpretations must be integrated before the major issue can be articulated most accurately.

How the major issue is handled—the second consideration—can be determined in two ways. The simplest method, when the clinician uses the EMP (see Chapter 5), is to chart the pleasantness ratings (pages 9 and 10) from the EMP. These ratings should provide a preliminary objective assessment of how well the individual is coping with the major issue as each successive EM is recalled. The second approach is to make an independent assessment of whether each memory appears to be healthy and to note changes from the beginning of the EM series to the end. The patterns that emerge from these analyses are described in principle 2 below.

A positive or healthy EM from a Cognitive-Perceptual viewpoint typically manifests at least one of the following characteristics: (a) the focus in the EM is on a positive interaction with another person in conjunction with the strongest affect being positive; (b) a problem or obstacle posed early in the memory has been overcome at the end (see Eisenhower's first memory earlier in the chapter); (c) the afterthought following the recollection of a generally negative EM reflects learning, an increase in coping skills or increased determination (see Golda Meir's first memory). A negative EM is characterized by at least one of the following: (a) a destructive interaction with another person that is not favorably resolved; (b) a failed mastery experience; (c) a loss occurring, such as a death or move; (d) an avoidant response to a stressful situation; (e) evidence of significant defects in reality testing or bad judgment; (f) indications of significant problems with impulse control.

Two general principles emerge in the process interpretation of EMs.

1. How an individual begins a series of EMs depicts his initial manner of self-presentation. Thus, the first EM is apt to reflect how the person is most likely to present himself in an interpersonal interaction.

2. How the EM series unfolds holds important diagnostic information. Five types of basic patterns are discernible:

A. The set of memories begins positively but deteriorates as new memories are given. Such individuals present well at first but lack the inner resources to sustain this impression. On a Rorschach protocol, analysts describe the equivalent pattern in terms of an erosion of defenses.

B. The memories begin poorly but improve as new memories are given. The prognosis in this case is better than when the situation is reversed. Such memories suggest that the individual is presently encountering difficulties but has the resources available to resolve the problem. The later EMs provide reassurance and often solutions to the original problem. They often remind the individual to persevere in spite of difficulties, with the knowledge that these problems can be resolved, just as earlier problems were confronted and resolved.

C. Memories involving good and bad outcomes cycle in a manner that is similar to a sine wave function. If such cycling occurs, an uneven pattern of strengths and weaknesses is reflected. Such patterns frequently reflect parallel affective disturbances consistent with such diagnoses as manic depressive disorder, borderline personality, and cyclothymic personality.

D. Things remain bad throughout the series of memories. In a clinical population, this pattern is quite common. Such memories usually reflect deficits in coping mechanisms, poor object relations, a negative view of the self and the world, a depressed mood, or some combination of the above. When all apply, to an extreme extent, the prognosis is much less favorable than when only one or two aspects apply, and then only to a minor extent.

E. Things remain good throughout the series of memories. Such an outcome occurs rarely, even for successful, well-functioning individuals. More common is a pattern in which a series of problems is posed and resolved in a set of early memories. Such an EM set reflects an abundance of coping skills (see Eisenhower's first memory earlier in the chapter). A series of very positive EMs in a clinical sample in conjunction with a passive self-presentation (e.g., Christmases and birthday parties in which gifts are received) typically reflects either a narcissistic orientation (wanting to be special/receiving effortless gratification) or an over-idealization of the past, consistent with a depressed mood.

The following set of EMs illustrates a Type A EM set with Type C aspects. Interpretive comments that follow each memory deal with its contents from a Cognitive-Perceptual viewpoint but emphasize process as the associations flow from one memory to the next. This subject is a nineteen-year-old single white male. The memories reflect depression, problems with impulse control, and self-destructive tendencies. The flow of associations from one memory to the next is particularly interesting and provides us with a graphic picture of his issues as well as his usual defenses.

Earliest Childhood Memories

EM 1

As far back as I can? I was four. I used to play with my real father. I had a big green dinosaur. Its head used to go up and down. (What is clearest in the memory?) The dinosaur. I used to love it. I'd turn it on, and it'd go walking around the apartment. (Are you remembering a particular time?) When I was visiting my real father. My mother had already divorced him. That's the last thing I remember about him. (What is the strongest feeling in the memory?) Happy—to be with him. We used to barbeque on the balcony. I used to love doing that.

Precis: "I need to be with my father."
Affiliation needs (see Glossary of Needs) are prominent in this memory. Most particularly, we sense a strong need to connect with a strong, paternal figure. The contact that he remembers, however, is relatively distant—being in a place together, as opposed to doing something with each other and interacting. The focal point in the memory is a big green dinosaur, which may symbolize his jealousy (the color green) and his anger (dinosaurs are huge, frightening animals) about losing his father.

EM 2

And I had an erector set. I used to make a robot. A walking robot. . . . They're just starting to come out with them again. (Are you remembering a particular time?) No. That's fifteen years ago. (What is the strongest feeling in the memory?) That I could do it on my own. That I was smart. (You were by yourself?) My dad helped me a little bit. But I did it mostly on my own. Me and my dad used to play together with that. That is as far back as I can remember 'cause after that my dad married.

Precis: "I remember making something on my own—with a little help from my dad."
This memory focuses on achievement and affiliation needs. The choice

of making a walking robot as a mastery task may be significant in that a robot is controlled and has no feelings. A walking robot may symbolize what he believes he is supposed to become if he is to please his father. His striving for independence is also noteworthy. He comments that he felt good about working on his own, suggesting that emancipation is an ongoing issue for him ("My dad helped me a little bit"). The vagueness of his memories is also striking; both may be reports (recollections of repeated events), as opposed to memories of specific one-time events. Whether or not they are reports, they appear to be highly idealized pictures of how he would have liked his childhood to have been. Idealization of the past is usually associated with depressive mood. At the end of the memory, he raises another depressive theme—he notes the loss of his father through remarriage, which raises questions as to his willingness to make deep attachments. In terms of his current situation, he is preoccupied with losing his adoptive father, who is in his late sixties and in somewhat fragile health.

EM 3

And my dad had this T-bird, and I used to ride around in the back seat. I used to look out of this porthole window all the time. (Are you recalling a particular time?) No. (What is the strongest feeling in the memory?) Looking out the window and seeing a red brick apartment area. Like I am waiting for somebody. Looking out and seeing a little emblem on the window. We had a third-floor apartment, a two-bedroom apartment in B———. His car was blue.

Precis: "I remember waiting for someone."

In this memory, affiliation needs again emerge. He remembers waiting for someone, likely his father. A symbolic separation has occurred. Metaphorically, he feels that he takes a back seat to his father, suggesting feelings of worthlessness as well as feelings of abandonment (father is not there). As his associations continue from his second memory, he appears to be feeling a sense of loss although he denies having any feelings whatsoever.

EM 4

After my dad—after I stopped seeing him. Living in B———. Riding my bike with my friends, being a kid. I don't remember anything specific. (See if you can remember something specific.) We had a big St. Bernard that I loved when my sister was born [to his mother's second marriage]. The dog kept knocking her over and hurting her. (What is clearest in the memory?) Me walking around with the dog. Its name was Bulldozer. (What is the strongest feeling in the memory?) I hated to see it go.

Precis: "I felt bad to lose my dog."

In this memory, we find evidence of an underlying depression. In the preceding memories, the client has been attempting to ward off feelings of loss by recalling times that he and his father were together, however tenuous that connection might be. The St. Bernard, who serves as a stand-in for the client, acts out his anger at being overthrown by his sister. In addition, the dog's leaving mirrors his feelings of loss over his father. This material is presented symbolically, not directly, an indication that he continues to try to block these feelings from awareness.

EM 5

We had a dog named Blackie. It got hit on the beltway. It committed suicide. It went on the beltway and a tractor trailer ran it over. I couldn't do nothing but stand there and watch. I couldn't believe that the dog wouldn't listen to me. I was screaming at it. For some reason the dog wouldn't listen to me. It just laid right down on the beltway and got run over. I was about six or seven. (What is clearest in the memory?) Hmm. Me and R. screaming, "Get an ambulance, get an ambulance." Tried to get someone to help us. We just ran down there to that highway in the maid's car. The dog was lying there dead. I don't know why I remember this, but I remember one ripped ear and crying.

That is the only major tragedy that I remember in my childhood. When it got hit, it got thrown in the air. It was gross. I couldn't believe it. That dog did everything I told it to do. It was *mine*. My dog. My dad tried to get another dog, but it wasn't the same.

Precis: "I felt helpless and out of control when my dog committed suicide."

In this memory we experience, full force, the feelings of depression associated with the loss of his father. Blackie, through his actions, reflects the client's feelings of loss and his resultant, self-destructive actions. Like Blackie, the client, too, does not listen. He is also headstrong. The memory thus serves as a warning. The memory also reflects his tremendous need to control (see Dominance in the Glossary), and it plays out graphically the implications of losing control. We also see, through the placement of this memory in the sequence, how defended he is against depression. Only gradually do these feelings emerge in the course of eliciting an extended set of recollections.

EM 6

Riding my minibike when I was twelve. My sister got a horse. I would say this was five years later. There was things in between, but I am just thinking of the big things that happened. I'm on top of the world. (What is clearest in the memory?) Riding my minibike around the back yard. It was yellow. I was happy. Everybody in the neighborhood had a minibike but me. Then I had one, and I was happy. (What is the strongest feeling in the memory?) Happy.

Precis: "After everyone else got one, I finally got a minibike."
Although this memory spotlights feelings of deprivation ("Everybody in the neighborhood had one but me"), it also offers hope as he was eventually able to get what he wanted. This memory also expresses his concerns about being different, about being left out, and his wish to be included. Historically, the memory hints that some recovery has been made from the depression associated with the loss of his father.

EM 7

Moving. (What do you recall about this?) Moving out to A. Road where my [step]dad lives now. I was happy. I had a horse. I could go hunting. Riding on the property. Going to the horse shows. Everything going great! Everything! (What is clearest in the memory?) Getting a nice big bedroom. Getting a gun to go hunting. My own horse. I still got the horse. Matter of fact, it's the best horse on the farm. Everything was going great. (What was your age at the time of the memory?) Oh, my God—that was when I was eleven.

I don't know how old I told you I was when I got the minibike. I was nine when I got the minibike cause I still had it when we moved.

Precis: "After we moved, I got a horse, the best one on the farm."
The sixth memory suggested some competitive feelings with his sister—she got a horse while he got a minibike for a gift. In his seventh memory, he wins—he not only gets a horse, it is the "best horse" on the farm. We thus see a gradual transition from a preoccupation with losses and deprivation to competitive feelings, particularly with his sister. He appears to be preoccupied with his place in his stepfather's affection, a natural concern since his biological father dropped out of his life and his stepfather now has a daughter of his own. He seems to be wondering, "How much does my dad really love me now that he had a child of his own?" He appears to answer this question for himself, via his seventh

memory, by enumerating his gifts, but the manner in which he responds suggests considerable denial.

EM 8

Starting to mess up in high school, junior high. Meeting the wrong people. (What is the clearest in the memory?) Just messing up. School grades dropping. That is why I started doing drugs. About a year after we moved in. I've always had that tendency—to find a bad crowd instead of a good crowd. (How do you understand that?) It always seemed like you were in charge. We always picked on the smart people. But the brainy people never picked on us. A lot of them kids knew who I was. They kidded me about being a spoiled rich kid. So I was a hell-raiser. I just caused problems. I was always getting into trouble. If I had it to do over, I would just be one of the kids that went to school and didn't get into trouble.

In EM 7, he finally appears to reach the point he wanted—he is valuable and important. In EM 8, he falls off the proverbial mountain. The memory suggests that he cannot take the pressure and demands associated with getting older—more challenging studies, more homework. His memory indicates that he felt "dumb," as he differentiates himself from the "smart people" in his school. Feelings of inadequacy are implied, as well as a fear of failure. Perhaps he felt unable to attract his father's attention by being successful so he got attention by acting out.

It should be noted that many of these recollections may not be EMs per se—EMs 1, 2, 3, 4, 6, 7, and 8 are all questionable. Only EM 5 is indisputably a memory of a one-time event, and this is the most traumatic recollection in the set. The lack of specific early memories suggests either severe repression, a lack of psychological mindedness, a disinterest in reflection, or some combination of the above in a non-organically impaired individual with average or better intelligence.

The memories as a group, following the Cognitive-Perceptual interpretive method, indicate a mixed self-presentation: strong feelings of inadequacy despite some competencies, and fears of failing in an action-oriented individual with strong achievement and affiliation needs. This young man feels best about himself when he is active, in control, engaged in mastery activities, and an accepted member of a respected peer group. Having status and feeling accepted are important considerations. He feels worst—likely quite depressed and discouraged—when he feels rejected, isolated, abandoned, or when he perceives himself as failing or not in control. At such times he is at risk to abuse substances to escape his depression.

He sees others as unreliable and inconsistent. He is apprehensive about establishing close ties because of his fears of rejection and abandonment. He is still oriented toward people, however, but he is more likely to associate with a counterculture group because he believes that he is not good enough.

When he is not depressed, he views the world around him as interesting and exciting, full of possibilities. Although he is oriented toward achieving and mastery, he is easily discouraged when things become difficult and is inclined to give up, partly due to his low self-esteem.

The major issue for this young man on an interpersonal level is establishing and maintaining satisfying personal relationships. On an intrapsychic level, he is trying to establish his independence and self-reliance while he emancipates from his family. With regard to his family, there appears to be a disturbance in his relationship with his stepfather and an accompanying wish to repair that relationship. But his ambivalence about working on his relationship with his stepfather (and his father) have made it difficult to separate from the family and become emotionally independent.

The goal of this chapter was to introduce the interpretation of EMs, reports, family myths, and other autobiographical memories with the Cognitive-Perceptual method. A brief introduction to the process interpretation of a set of memories was also provided. The next chapter will present the EMP and discuss its unique contributions to the assessment of autobiographical memory. Under ordinary circumstances, the EMP is regarded as the procedure of choice in assessing autobiographical memory.

NOTES

1. An attempt was made to verify the factual aspects of this memory via the client's mother. Although the mother confirmed that her daughter was a difficult child, she did not recall being invited to a governor's ball or any facsimile of the event in question. This example illustrates well the fantasy aspect of many EMs.

2. The following material concerning Eisenhower's first EM is a revised version of a paper by Bruhn and Bellow (1984) that originally appeared in the *Journal of Personality Assessment* and was subsequently modified slightly by Bruhn (1984). The writer is grateful to the *Journal of Personality Assessment* and Jossey-Bass for permission to use this material.

3. This section contains an adapted version of a chapter by Bruhn and Bellow (1987) entitled, "The Cognitive-Perceptual Approach to the Interpretation of Early Memories: The Earliest Memories of Golda Meir," which is used with the permission of Lawrence Erlbaum Associates.

4. This section is a revised version of material that originally appeared in a paper by Bruhn (1985). Permission from the *Journal of Personality Assessment* to use this material is appreciated.

5

THE COGNITIVE-
PERCEPTUAL MODEL AND
THE EARLY MEMORIES
PROCEDURE

What disturbs men's minds is not events but their judgments on
events.

Epictetus

It was apparent as I began working with EMs that a standardized, formal
means to assess autobiographical memory was needed if our understanding of autobiographical memory and its clinical applications was to advance. I therefore began to experiment with various written forms to
test their effectiveness. These initial explorations raised an increasingly
perplexing question: How should a projective assessment of autobiographical memory be undertaken?

One approach, which derives from the Adlerian tradition, is to request
only EMs from before age eight. If this option is used, the clinician must
decide how many EMs to request (one? the first five?). There are at least
three major liabilities with this approach, however. The first is that some
people do not recall any specific events from before age eight. The
second is that many clients tend to become side-tracked as to when a
memory occurred and whether it in fact occurred before age eight,
thereby disrupting the flow of associations. The third is that many psychologically significant, and perhaps critical events, occur after age eight
(the break up of a marriage, a rape, the loss of a significant other).

I chose to resolve the first and second problems, perhaps somewhat
arbitrarily, by requesting the earliest memory and the next four memories that come to mind by association. This approach does not dispatch
these problems directly but skirts them by requesting the earliest rec-

ollection and others that flesh out the issue uncovered by the first (through association).

The third problem—significant events that occurred after age eight—remains unresolvable in any EM-based assessment of autobiographical memories. Since I wanted to assess the whole of autobiographical memory, I decided to attack the problem from two directions. First, I asked for the clearest or most important memory/lifetime (see *EMP*, Memory 6). This approach put no artificial limits or constraints on a client's choice of memory. The page for additional memories follows in the same vein. Second, I probed categories of memories that I was confident, from my clinical experience and research with EMs, would yield psychological gold. These included categories such as most traumatic memory, a memory of an inappropriate sexual experience, and a memory of a parent using drugs or alcohol. The problem with relying on *directed* memories is that any given category may be empty. For instance, if asked for the most important memory of being punished, a client might respond that she does not recall ever being punished aside from mild rebukes and that nothing specific comes to mind. Because such probes may yield nothing, directed memories (see Part II, *EMP*) are used to effectively rule out common clinical issues. The client who denies having had an inappropriate sexual experience or who denies any clear memories of punishment is unlikely to have issues associated with either matter. The presence of numerous such memories or several vivid ones, on the other hand, strongly suggests that there are important issues to be processed in these areas although the priority of such issues remains an open question. For example, issues involving a past history of sexual abuse are likely to be quite significant, but they may not be priorities relative to the issues raised in the spontaneous memories in Part I.

The decision to develop a written procedure to assess autobiographical memory was prompted by the following considerations.

1. Clients report almost to a person that they feel more comfortable disclosing problematic memories on paper than with their therapist. The most common reasons given for not disclosing such information in session are:

   A. They were too embarrassed to say anything; or

   B. The therapist made no inquiry as to whether they had had these kinds of experiences.

This finding is consistent with reports that suggest many clients feel more comfortable disclosing embarrassing information to a computer than to a clinician face-to-face.

2. The EMP provides clients with an opportunity to engage in a structured life review. This process enables clients to ponder aspects of

their past that are critical to their work in therapy. The procedure is designed to help clients gain an awareness of the self and current life issues early in the treatment process.

3. Perhaps more than any other test or procedure, the EMP provides a novice psychotherapy client with a practical introduction to insight-oriented psychotherapy. It instructs by example as to what the treatment process is like so that clients who are naive about the process of psychotherapy can be self-taught by completing the EMP.

4. The EMP saves considerable clinician time at the beginning of therapy by probing routine matters in a cost-efficient, systematic manner. By the end of the second session, client and therapist can be reasonably clear about the underlying basis for such common presenting complaints as anxiety, depression, feeling empty, and so on. As a result, the process of working on and resolving the problem can begin earlier in the therapeutic process. Those clients who are affected by financial, insurance, or other reality constraints and who can tolerate a focused, short-term therapy can be helped more quickly because the therapist does not need to gather data that the EMP can collect.

WORKING WITH WRITTEN VERSUS ORAL EARLY MEMORIES

Many writers have commented that clients enjoy sharing their EMs with an examiner. It is generally observed that the process of obtaining EMs from individuals is much less threatening than completing other projective tasks such as the Rorschach. My experience is consistent with these observations. I estimate that individuals who become at least moderately upset in the process of disclosing their EMs to an interviewer comprise less than five percent of a college population and probably less than ten percent of a psychiatric outpatient population.

Completing the Early Memories Procedure, however, involves a much different process than sharing a set of spontaneous EMs with an examiner. Consider the following quantifiable or concrete differences: (1) the EMP requires more client time, typically about two and a half to four hours versus twenty to thirty minutes for EMs obtained orally; (2) the EMP requests fifteen directed EMs of various kinds which most interview formats do not explore, and some of the directed EMs probe areas that are troublesome for many clients (traumas, inappropriate sexual experiences); (3) the EMP asks the client to interpret one of his EMs and to discuss why he thinks he recalled what he did, neither of which commonly occurs in interview formats. The major differences between the oral EMs procedure and the EMP are summarized in Table 5.1.

Table 5.1
Differences Between the EMP and EMs Obtained Orally

	Oral EMs	EMP
Age/Skills Required	Must be 5 to 7 years or older. Some 5, 6, or 7 year olds may not be testable if IQ or verbal ability is low.	Requires the equivalent of 4th grade writing skills or dictating equipment if writing skills are poor.
Exclusionary Criteria	Not appropriate for individuals who are actively psychotic or easily prone to psychotic episodes. Most individuals can produce at least a few EMs unless they are severely repressed or extremely unreflective. Some with poor verbal skills or low intellectual ability may also experience difficulty.	(Same as for oral EMs but in addition . . .) Some individuals with severe attention and concentration problems, certain organic difficulties, severe depression or anxiety, or very weak defenses (e.g., poorly functioning borderlines) may not be able to complete the *EMP*, especially in an acute episode. Generally speaking, individuals who can complete an MMPI can usually complete the *EMP*.
Time Required	Obtaining a set of 5 to 10 EMs requires about 30 minutes of face-to-face time.	Orienting an individual requires about 5 minutes of face-to-face time at the end of the intake interview. Most individuals require 2 1/2 to 4 hours on their own to complete the *EMP*.
Intensity of Affective Experience	The affective experience is predominantly positive and usually subdued relative to the *EMP*.	The affective experience is reported to be much more intense and negative by individuals who have shared their EMs orally and subsequently completed the EMP. Their explanations for the greater intensity include: (1) they had more time to complete the *EMP*; (2) they were not distracted by the examiner's reactions and were more involved with the task when they worked by themselves.

Table 5.1 (continued)

	Oral EMs	EMP
Reaction to the Task	Most individuals enjoy talking about their EMs and respond positively to the task even when their EMs are moderately negative.	Most individuals report that they learn a great deal about themselves and comment that writing about their memories helps them to access their feelings. Most experience the *EMP* as "inviting" although a significant minority experience it as "imposing" or "intimidating," primarily due to the length.
What Individuals Learn from the Task	Most individuals evidence minimal understanding of what their EMs reveal about them.	A sample of 20 outpatients were asked to rate on a 5-point scale how much they learned about themselves from taking the *EMP*. The mean score was 2.9 (a "fair amount"), while the mode was 4 (a "moderate amount").

For a variety of reasons, many individuals report difficulty completing the EMP. In one informal study, I found that approximately forty percent of my outpatients took at least three weeks to finish the EMP. About twenty percent were so resistant that several months were required before they completed the procedure. Approximately ten percent never did. For example, one bright, articulate woman, who had previously been in treatment for over ten years with several eminent therapists, stated that she could not complete the procedure. The reason became clear as we discussed her response to the task. The process of completing the procedure, she said, dredged up many painful memories that she had never shared with anyone, not even her therapists. Nor was she willing to face these memories now. How to minimize the probability of resistance is discussed in the next section.

What are some of the less obvious differences between the EMP and EMs obtained in an interview? The latter involves a more superficial process psychologically. Typically, five or fewer spontaneous EMs are obtained, and it is easier for the client to avoid significant material when he has to produce only a small number of EMs. But there are two differences between the EMP and EM interview that seem to be key. First, the EMP is completed in private. The EMP thus requires more of an introspective and reflective process than oral EMs. In a sense, self-disclosure never becomes an issue—in a written format the client talks to himself. Second, and probably more important, the EMP explicitly requests traumatic memories. Clients are usually willing to reveal such material to a therapist, but they often must be explicitly asked to do so. If they are not asked, many clients will not voluntarily disclose traumatic material. The lesson appears to be, "If you want to know, ask."

There are subtle aspects to the EMP that add to its uniqueness. Many clients talk about how different it feels to commit their memories to paper. For them it makes the events more real. They report that they focus more on what happened and as they do, the feelings in the memories become more intense. Many remark that when they present a memory in session their attention is diverted from their feelings and from the deeper meaning of the events that they are recounting. They wonder how the therapist is reacting, or they may worry about losing control in the session. Alone and freed from the distraction of the therapy relationship, they can immerse themselves in the memory and focus solely on their experience of the event.

Completing the EMP can be compared to writing an autobiography about one's most significant life experiences. Many clients report that the procedure enabled them to come to terms with major life experiences. In contrast, recounting one's EMs to a therapist is much like telling stories, which is fun for most people. However, the same "stories" on paper feel different as the individual accesses fragments that were overlooked and feelings that had receded into the background of a memory recounted in session. A Gestalt phenomenon also appears to operate in that the whole becomes more than the sum of the parts. As the individual works with many of the highlights of his life—twenty-one or more memories—he begins to see patterns. He is asked how he might like to change some of his experiences. He is asked to identify his most significant EMs and explain why they are significant to him. He is asked to interpret a memory. Such questions help clients to assess material that may have gone unexamined for much of their adult lives. For many clients, taking the EMP precipitates a profound emotional experience, one that helps to build the motivation needed for insight-oriented psychotherapy. Further, working on the EMP helps clients to better understand insight-oriented therapy by providing them with an object lesson and an overview of material that they will need to work through.

Perhaps one of the strongest and most eloquent testimonials for the use of written memories comes from the eminent analyst, Helene Deutsch, one of Freud's earliest disciples. Deutsch (1973) discovered the power of writing down her memories in the process of completing her autobiography.

> Autobiography is a process that is under firmer self-control than the analytic method of free association. For that reason I am amazed at how often memories I recognize as long buried beyond the reach

of consciousness—yes, memories that have even eluded psychoanalysis—readily come back without any serious resistance as I write
my autobiography. . . .

I have learned during this writing that even given the sincerest
effort to be objective, each memory is shaped more or less by one's
current psychic condition, as well as by this memory's continuing
influence on one's life as a whole. Sometimes a minute incident,
harmless in itself, acquires in one's memory a lasting significance.
. . .

From such recollections I have, strange to say, sometimes learned
more about myself than from psychoanalysis. (p. 15)

My experience with the EMP confirms Deutsch's. The EMP simply
provides a more structured means to accessing key memories than attempting an autobiography.

INTRODUCING THE EARLY MEMORIES PROCEDURE AND MINIMIZING RESISTANCE

It is recommended that the EMP can be completed after intake by
clients who do not meet the exclusionary criteria (see Table 5.1). The
EMP may be introduced as follows:

We have discussed some of the problems and issues that have
brought you into treatment. We have not had much of an opportunity, though, to talk about your early years, your family, and
some of your more important life experiences. To save time, I
would like to suggest that you take home something that will help
us review this information. Otherwise, this is likely to take us some
time, and I know that you are impatient to start working on *x* [the
client's presenting problem or complaint]. How does that sound?

At the end of the initial intake session, most clients are maximally
motivated to resolve their presenting problem. They are willing to do
anything reasonable to facilitate that process.

Some clients, however, may have already begun treatment when you
decide to obtain an EMP. How can such clients be approached? One of
the following introductions may be helpful:

1. [For the client who has already grown considerably] You have grown
   considerably since we first started working. Often, when a lot of
   change takes place, new issues come up that were not prominent in
   the beginning. I use the EMP to understand these issues, so I am

wondering if you would be willing to take this home with you and fill it out.

2. [For the client who is not making any progress or who seems to be getting worse] I have been thinking a lot about your situation, and I am concerned that there might be something that both of us have overlooked. So I am wondering if you would be willing to take this home with you and fill it out.

Most clients are receptive to the idea of undertaking a life review. Nevertheless, it is not uncommon for clients to express or act out resistance as they begin to work on the procedure.

Previewing the EMP to the client is the best way to minimize the likelihood of resistance. Begin by asking the client to read the instructions for Part I and for the first EM. Ask the client whether she has any questions. If not, nothing further is needed. Some clients, however, are not certain what is meant by an EM. If so, ask the client for her first EM. If her response meets the criteria for an EM, reinforce it: "Yes, that's exactly what I'm looking for. It's a memory of a specific event, something that happened at one time." If the client still seems uncertain, suggest that she continue to the next page. Previewing two EMs is sufficient for most clients.

When the process of previewing is complete, state to the client:

When you write down your memories, it may be that exactly the same memories will come to mind. However, some people report that they recall different memories. It does not matter whether you remember the same memories or new memories, either one is fine. Most people report that it takes them at least two hours to complete the EMP. Can you set aside that much time before we meet next?

After the therapist has previewed the procedure with the client, and the client has committed herself to complete it, the probability that resistance will occur has been reduced to an absolute minimum.

At the beginning of the second session, ask the client what her experience was with the EMP. Was she surprised by what she remembered? Did any questions cause her difficulties? If the client was able to complete the EMP, a debriefing period will help to determine what the client's problem areas are. If she was not able to finish certain parts, the basis for her difficulty can be determined. On the other hand, if the client did not do any work on the EMP, her reason must be addressed and discussed.

CLIENT RESISTANCE TO THE EARLY MEMORIES PROCEDURE

The clinician may expect resistance from many clients when they are asked to complete the EMP. Three kinds have been observed. The first is the response that one encounters from busy, harried, impatient, or troubled individuals when they are asked to undertake a lengthy and challenging task. The most effective way to deal with this type of resistance is to acknowledge the client's feelings but to stress that the procedure should help to streamline the therapy process by pinpointing important events and developing an overview of her life that otherwise would consume many sessions. Most clients will agree to complete the procedure once their complaints have been understood and accepted. After clients begin the task, most become engaged and need no further prodding.

The second kind of resistance is pathological. Consider the following examples. One woman who had been in treatment with several previous therapists took weeks to complete the EMP. Finally, the therapist confronted her. She stated that she was stuck on several types of memories. One involved being beaten by her older brother nearly every day for a number of years, and another concerned a series of painful sexual memories. She stated that she had never discussed these matters in therapy before and that she was having trouble because every time she started writing she was overwhelmed with feelings. The same avoidant pattern was played out with each of her previous therapists—she talked about what she felt comfortable talking about and avoided what was painful until she became disillusioned with therapy and quit.

Another client was referred for marital therapy after several years of individual work. In this instance, he and his wife both resisted completing the procedure. The husband categorically refused to look at his past. He initially claimed that he had no EMs, which meant, as it turned out later, that he did not want to have any EMs. Because his past contained many painful events, he chose to deal only with the here and now in his individual treatment until he was urged in couples therapy to look at these matters. In his wife's case, her self-esteem was closely tied up with "getting things done." The process of completing the EMP thus presented two problems: (1) when she worked on the EMP she could not finish things that "were important" which made her feel worthless and depressed; and (2) her EMs consisted primarily of "failure experiences," which made her feel worthless and inadequate when she focused on them. The preceding examples suggest that client resistance to the EMP can be treated in the same manner as any other resistance in therapy. It is important to help the client understand what he is avoiding and to find some means to confront it. If the therapist aligns himself with the client in avoiding the cause of the resistance, the client is likely to tap dance around the issues that brought him to treatment with little resulting improvement.

The third kind of resistance involves the clinician's ambivalence about the procedure. Some clinicians feel uncomfortable about asking clients to participate in their own treatment, especially if the task requires effort. They may feel more comfortable, for instance, dispensing medications to make the client feel better. In this way they can function in a nurturing and supportive role. Using an instrument like the EMP requires that the therapist function as a teacher or guide: "Let's try *x* and see what we can learn from it." Therapists who worry about asking their clients to become more active in their treatment because they want to protect their clients are often uncomfortable initially with the EMP.

Clients who refuse the procedure, or parts thereof, are communicating by their resistance that they may not be ready to come to terms with certain aspects of their lives. If so, this resistance, like any other, becomes something to explore.

THE EARLY MEMORIES PROCEDURE AND THE ASSESSMENT OF OBJECT RELATIONS

It is apparent that every projective technique must tap autobiographical memory—at least indirectly—if it is to succeed in assessing personality. How is it, then, that we have failed to devise a methodology to understand the self and its conflicts? Most of us would recoil at the thought of measuring intelligence through responses to story cards or ink blots, although both provide a useful adjunctive perspective on some aspects of intellectual functioning. Fortunately, there are better methods to assess intellectual ability than by story cards. Exactly the same argument obtains in the case of autobiographical memory.

From another perspective, what we say about an individual's object relations from a Rorschach protocol presupposes that he has an autobiographical memory, that he perceives significant objects in a paradigmatic ways, and that he interacts with them accordingly. In my experience, however, it is a far simpler task to assess autobiographical memory directly than to use Rorschach data to ferret out this information indirectly. For instance, if we want to make specific inferences about an individual's schema for his mother, why not ask him for his first memory of his mother; his most important memory of his mother; his clearest memory of his mother; his happiest memory of his mother; and his most traumatic memory involving his mother? If we want to make inferences about an individual's schema of his mother from Rorschach data, we are forced to make inferences from such data as his low number of human movement responses, the fact that he saw a spider on Card 1, the quality of his responses to Card 7, etc. This is not to argue that such inferences are invalid. Quite the contrary. A Samuel Beck, Bruno Klopfer, John Exner, or Paul Lerner can do magical things with a Rorschach protocol. The point is this: Why cut down a tree with an ax when you can use a chainsaw? In my opinion, it is much easier to assess object relations with autobiographical memories than Rorschach data or any other kind of projective data for that matter.

Nothing that has been said thus far should be construed as an attack upon the Rorschach. I personally use the Rorschach along with the Early Memories Procedure and believe that both instruments have their unique place in the study of personality. At the same time, I would argue that it is a wrongheaded and perverse use of the Rorschach—or any projective technique for that matter—to employ it in roles in which it is not especially well-suited. But if the clinician wishes to assess object relations, the Early Memories Procedure is by far the most reasonable choice. The Rorschach can be used for cross-validation purposes, but the assessment of object relations is not its forte.

OTHER TESTS OF AUTOBIOGRAPHICAL MEMORY

Perhaps the most frequent comment that I hear from mental health professionals when I introduce the EMP is, "Why do we need the EMP? Don't we already assess autobiographical memory?" This question is generally followed with an example of how the clinician believes he is using a particular technique or series of probes to assess some aspect of autobiographical memory. An easy way to address this question is to consider some common examples.

Many psychologists argue that they assess autobiographical memory with standard personality tests. The classical procedures (Rorschach, TAT) tap autobiographical memory indirectly by trying to induce perceptual distortions. With the exception of EMs, which tap only a small part of autobiographical memory, no other standard technique has been used to make a direct assessment.

By far the most frequent response, however, comes from the clinician who says, "I always ask my clients, 'Tell me about your childhood, your mother, your father, and so forth.' It seems to me that there isn't much difference between that and what you are asking on the EMP." To illustrate the difference, I respond by asking: "What do your clients say when you ask them these questions?" If we are referring to individuals at intake who previously have not been in insight-oriented psychotherapy, the clinician generally smiles sheepishly and acknowledges that the information was not very useful. In the case of "Tell me about your father," some bland, socially appropriate adjectives usually follow: "He was a hardworking man, good provider, quiet, always there for us when we needed him." Such questions are usually a waste of time since they call for conclusions based on data so far removed from autobiographical memory that it is difficult to know what we are getting—it could be what he was told as a child by his parents to tell outsiders if they asked. When we ask broad questions that call for conclusions, judgments, or opinions from clients, that is exactly the type of response that we are likely to obtain—but conclusions, judgments, and opinions are several steps removed from the events stored in autobiographical memory. Better that the clinician return to the data itself than ask the client for opinions or conclusions that may, upon closer inspection, be orthogonal to his experience.

Perhaps the most common clinical error in assessing autobiographical memory is, as was just discussed, to ask questions that pull for opinions such as, "What was your father like?" A second frequent error involves asking questions that pull for conclusions such as, "How was punishment handled in your family?" Notice that the question implicitly requires that the client scan all family memories in autobiographical memory related to punishment of the self and siblings and provide a summary response reflective of this universal set of memories. Do clients actually go through this process? With rare exceptions, no. If not, what do they do? When I asked individuals how they process this type of question, most stated that they had a mental picture or series of pictures flash before them. Sometimes these pictures are based upon actual one-time events, and sometimes they are associated with a composite impression of how their parents handled punishment situations. If we are interested in how punishment was *often* handled, "How was punishment handled in your family?" is an appropriate probe. However, if we want to know whether the individual has unresolved issues related to punishment, this is not the best question to ask. The proper assessment of autobiographical memory would be: "What is your earliest memory of being punished? What are your clearest or most important memories of being punished? and What is your most distressing memory of being punished?"

A third error is common even among sophisticated graduate and psychiatric training programs: requesting that a student give an overview of his life or an era from his life. To help the student conduct a self-study, he is asked variously to write an autobiography of thirty pages or so, to discuss his preschool years, his experience in elementary school, his adolescence, and so on. The reader is asked to consider how he would handle such a task. Most of us would begin by using a fairly conventional form: "I was born on (date) in (place). My parents were (names), and I had (number) brothers and (number) sisters." Notice that this form will emphasize dates, places, and numbers—orienting factual data—and later will focus on moves, if any, where the respondent went to school, how well he did in school, when he graduated, what childhood illnesses he contracted, and the like. As the preceding demonstrates, autobiographies tend to be historical records that contain factual data believed to be significant in the individual's culture.

If an autobiography is constructed to highlight a particular incident or set of incidents—which it usually is—such events almost invariably occur during adulthood and not before. If the reader samples a randomly selected group of autobiographies from the library, he will observe that most writers say relatively little about their pre-adult lives. The few who do still assume the role of historian, as opposed to an archeologist who wishes to examine and reflect upon specific happenings from his youth and thereby reconstructs that culture. Just as few writers of autobiographies recount recollections of specific events from their youth, so also is it true that few of us would respond with specific memories if asked about our past. For most of us, therefore, such requests indirectly tap aspects of autobiographical memory (the historical record), but they do not provide direct access to the information we seek.

If the clinician wishes to establish an historical record, then "Tell me about yourself" or "Tell me about your adolescence" are appropriate probes. If the clinician is concerned about unfinished business, however, this is not the best question to ask. The proper method to assess autobiographical memory would be "What are your clearest and most important memories?" (for an assessment of autobiographical memory, lifetime); "What are your clearest or most important memories of adolescence?" (for an assessment of adolescence). Other aspects of autobiographical memory can be explored as needed, for example, "What is your clearest or most important memory involving dating during adolescence?"

In sum, there is no adequate direct means to assess autobiographical memory except the Early Memories Procedure. Other commonly used probes and procedures tend to tap something other than autobiographical memory and therefore do not provide an adequate test. Most either make the error of pulling for opinions, soliciting conclusions without establishing an adequate data base, or accessing the historical record. The EMP avoids all three errors.

TYPES OF AUTOBIOGRAPHICAL MEMORIES

Upon closer inspection, we find that specific autobiographical memories can be grouped into three types. These include memories that:

1. preserve the original perceptions and original constructions (experience as originally processed);

2. preserve the original perceptions but include revised constructions (for instance as a result of successful psychotherapy); or

3. preserve neither the original perceptions nor constructions.

It is a simple matter to distinguish type 3 memories from types 1 and 2. If the client reports that he sees himself in the memory, the memory must be a type 3 since it would be impossible for an individual with an original perception (types 1 and 2) to see himself in the scene. Types 1 and 2 can be differentiated according to whether the construction in the memory is consistent with current beliefs, or whether it reflects an archaic understanding consistent with the age at which the memory occurred (see Milton Erickson's EMs). Most memories in an EMP are either types 2 or 3, with the latter predominating.

All three types are interpreted with the CP model in exactly the same manner. The differences among them are important only when we are interested in constructing a history. Type 3 memories are likely to be highly distorted derivatives of what actually happened; they are often complete fabrications. Types 1 and 2 are likely to portray events that actually occurred.

THE EARLY MEMORIES PROCEDURE AS A PROJECTIVE TECHNIQUE

Although most clinicians respond positively to the concept of assessing autobiographical memory, some question whether the EMP should be considered a projective test. Such objections typically involve the premise that autobiographical memory deals with real events ("facts"). These clinicians argue that facts should be regarded differently than fantasies or perceptions, which is the domain of "true" projective techniques. Such an argument implicitly assumes that: (1) memories are rarely if ever wrong or distorted; and (2) the recollection of past events conforms to the laws of memory and does not reflect the operation of personality.

That both assumptions are wrong can be easily demonstrated. Individuals with clear, sharp memories are the exception, not the rule, in our society. If autobiographical memory were organized in humans as it is in robots who are programmed to learn, facts would be accurate and distortions would be minimal. Identically manufactured robots would all "see things the same way," assuming equivalent experiences. However, people are not all manufactured the same way. They come from different cultures, they are raised by different families, and they are subjected to different life experiences. From these influences they acquire different values and attitudes and, ultimately, different ways of perceiving the world. It is therefore not surprising that different people often perceive the same event differently. These differences in perceptions are compounded when memories are subjected to the process of reconstruction. Whatever differences are present initially tend to expand, not contract, with time as data that is discrepant with the individual's belief system tends to be "forgotten." A robot that is unencumbered with political biases remembers facts about Republicans and Democrats equally well. Not so with human beings. Democrats tend to recall data that supports their political beliefs, as do Republicans. Neither tends to remember data that is damaging to their belief system. The same is generally true with individuals who are strict analysts or behaviorists, or followers of any "ism." If memory were organized in humans as it is in robots, it would be possible to decide with an absolute consensus who won a debate among presidential candidates, something that is not possible with the diversity of human perceptions.

The second assumption—that the recollection of past experience follows laws of memory and does not reflect the operation of personality—can be easily disproved. If this assumption were true, long-term autobiographical memory would not change when issues were resolved and personality was reorganized. But in point of fact, when issues are worked through, memories are reordered and revised. This premise is supported by data from a variety of research findings. For instance, Bach (1952) recorded all memories reported by his clients during the course of therapy. He demonstrated that memories related to issues which were resolved tended to be forgotten and disavowed by clients at the end of treatment. Several questionnaire studies categorized the content of EMs as a function of subjects' age, for example, Potwin (1901). All concluded that the content of EMs tends to shift with age. This pattern suggests that individuals tend to have developmentally appropriate concerns which are reflected in their selection of EMs. Eckstein (1976), on the other hand, compared pre- and post-treatment sets of EMs from a client in psychotherapy and concluded that her EMs reflected the changes in perspective that occurred as a result of psychotherapy. In each case, personality and developmental variables—more than the laws of memory—help us to understand what is retained and what is dropped from autobiographical memory.

If the recollection of events in autobiographical memory reflects the organization of personality, then there is warrant to conceptualize the EMP as a projective technique. Let us review the criteria that define a "projective technique." Rabin (Corsini, 1984) points out that although the term has been variously defined, the common denominators are contained in the following propositions:

1. Projective techniques present relatively ambiguous stimuli to the examinee.
2. The techniques are "response-free" in the sense that there are no

right or wrong responses and the examinee is free to give whatever responses appear suitable.

3. Responses are interpreted as reflecting central personality tendencies and affective states.

4. The obtained records are also viewed, in varying degrees, as reflections of the cognitive processes and personality style of the subject. (p. 78)

It is apparent by inspection that the EMP satisfies Rabin's four propositions with the possible exception of the first. Some who are accustomed to ambiguous picture cards or ink blots (visual stimuli) are confused by the EMP. What is ambiguous is the instructions to the subject, such as, "Think back to the earliest memory that you have." This instruction ("earliest") gives the individual considerable latitude in responding and therefore satisfies the ambiguity requirement in Rabin's definition.

There is little about the EMP that must be taken into account to understand the subject's response. For instance, with most projectives one must understand the stimulus pull for each part of the technique. Certain popular responses on the Rorschach are thought to have little significance because so many individuals report the percept. For example, a winged insect or a bat is so frequently reported on Card 5 that if a subject cannot see it during a testing of the limits, this would suggest an idiosyncracy in the perceptual process. On the EMP, there is no parallel need to determine the stimulus pull (note EMs 2 through 5), or the stimulus pull is explicitly indicated (for the sixth memory, a particularly clear or important memory). For the first five EMs, the EMP is as pure a projective test as could be devised.

THE EARLY MEMORIES PROCEDURE: ORGANIZATION AND PURPOSE

The EMP (see Table 5.2) consists of two major parts.[1] In Part I, six spontaneous EMs are requested; in Part II, fifteen directed memories of various kinds are elicited. Altogether, twenty-one memories are obtained, not including a page for additional memories. Other components of the EMP involve: (1) scales to rate the clarity and predominant affect of the six memories in Part I; (2) an instruction that directs the individual to rank order his most significant memories; (3) a question that requests the individual to explain why his most significant memories are significant for him; (4) an item that asks the individual to indicate the basis for his recalling the particular EMs he chose; (5) an instruction that directs the individuals to select one of his memories and to interpret it as best he can; (6) questions related to the individual's experience with the EMP, in addition to basic demographic data.

Table 5.2
Contents of the Early Memories Procedure

Page	Contents	Purpose of Probe
p. 1	Part I, Instructions	—
p. 2	Earliest Childhood Memory	Determine earliest memory
p. 3	Next Childhood Memory	Assemble a set of spontaneous EMs
p. 4	Next Childhood Memory	Assemble a set of spontaneous EMs
p. 5	Next Childhood Memory	Assemble a set of spontaneous EMs
p. 6	Next Childhood Memory	Assemble a set of spontaneous EMs
p. 7	A particularly *clear* or *important* memory from one's entire life	Assesses unresolved issues, lifetime; "Important" is deliberately ambiguous.
p. 8	Additional autobiographical memories—*lifetime*	Assesses *motivation* for the task, among other things
pp. 9-10	Rating scales for *clarity* and *pleasantness* for the first six memories.	Pleasantness ratings should correlate with *present mood*—i.e., a high level of unpleasant affect in EMs should correlate with *present* affective disturbance. Memories that are particularly *vivid* draw extra psychic energy, which suggests that they should be especially important.
p. 11	Rank order the three most significant EMs; explain why these memories are significant; explain why these particular EMs were recalled.	Assesses insight, ability to reflect and introspect, psychological mindedness
p. 13	Part II, Instructions	—
p. 14	First School Memory	Assesses attitudes toward achievement, mastery, independence
p. 15	First Punishment Memory	Assesses attitudes toward authority figures and fairness
p. 16	First Sibling Memory	Assesses sibling relationships, evidence of sibling rivalry
p. 17	First Family Memory	Assesses functioning in triadic or group situations
p. 18	Clearest Memory of Mother, Lifetime	Assesses relationship with mother, attitudes toward women
p. 19	Clearest Memory of Father, Lifetime	Assesses relationship with father, attitudes toward men
p. 20	A Memory of Someone You Admire, Lifetime	Assesses personal values and explores basis for potential role models
p. 21	Happiest Memory, Lifetime	Explores how strongest needs are best gratified
p. 22	Most Traumatic Memory, Lifetime	Elicits psychic injuries
p. 23	A Memory of Your Parents Fighting, Lifetime	Explores how conflict is likely to be processed

Table 5.2 (continued)

Page	Contents	Purpose of Probe
p. 24	A Memory of A Parent Involving Alcohol or Drugs, Lifetime	Probes whether individual has had to cope with a substance abusing parent and issues related to same
p. 25	An Incident That Made You Feel Most Ashamed, Lifetime	Explores issues involving guilt
p. 26	A Memory of Being Physically or Emotionally Abused, Childhood	Probes whether individual has a history of being abused and, if so, how
p. 27	A Memory of an Inappropriate Sexual Experience, Childhood or Adolescence	Probes whether individual has a history of sexual traumas
p. 28	A Fantasy Memory	Assesses the individual's strongest needs and how he would ideally like to meet these needs. Compare this response with that on happiest memory for "actual vs. ideal" gratification.
p. 29	An Interpretation of a Memory—Individual's Choice	Assesses psychological mindedness, ability to reflect and introspect, and helps to establish how the individual understands cause and effect in his life
pp. 30-31	Questionnaire—demographics, experience of and attitudes toward the *EMP*, time required to complete, the individual's beliefs about his EMs, and the individual's guess about the long-term reliability of his EMs.	Provides basic research data about the individual, the EMP, and EMs

Because the differences between spontaneous and directed memories are discussed in Volume II and in other papers (Bruhn, 1984; Bruhn & Schiffman, 1982a), a discussion of this matter will be abbreviated here. Suffice it to say that spontaneous EMs constitute a pure projective task. The first five EMs required on the EMP are spontaneous EMs. The first EM is the earliest and the next four are the EMs that come to mind by association. There is no attempt to restrict the selection of memories in any way other than by time ("earliest") and association ("next"), which are the criteria for a spontaneous memory. The directed memories (Table 5.2) are a mixed selection. Some are the earliest of a type (first EM of school, punishment, sibling), while others are the clearest memory from a lifetime (mother, father), while others still may be the most affectively potent or strongest of a type (an incident that made you feel ashamed) during one's lifetime. The choice of the type of probe (earliest versus clearest versus strongest) was made after several years of trying various approaches with colleagues and clients. Whatever seemed to yield the best results was used.

Whether directed EMs should be used in a projective test of autobiographical memory is debatable. The best argument for using spontaneous EMs exclusively is that one does not have to factor out the effect of the probe. As Bruhn and Schiffman (1982a) point out, if an individual is asked his favorite dessert and he answers, we know his favorite dessert. But if an individual is asked his favorite variety of ice cream, we will not know whether ice cream is his favorite dessert or even whether he likes ice cream. In a similar vein, some directed memories appear important, but they may concern matters that are trivial to the client. For instance, punishment may hold little present interest for a client, but he may readily produce a punishment memory if requested to do so. By contrast, we know that spontaneous EMs are important because if we argue the contrary—that spontaneous EMs have no meaning or value—we must also question the utility and adaptive value of long-term memory, both of which are well-established.

If spontaneous EMs are so significant, why use directed EMs at all? This is an excellent question. Early in my career, I did not request directed EMs. I then found that months or even years into their treatment, many clients began to report highly significant events that had never emerged previously in their spontaneous EMs: traumatic memories, memories of inappropriate sexual experiences, and so forth. When I requested such memories directly, many clients disclosed large numbers of traumatic, affect-laden memories that were not reported spontaneously. The issue of whether to include directed memories on the EMP was thus resolved empirically.

RELIABILITY

Although no separate study of the reliability of the EMP was undertaken, the reliability of EMs has been studied in several contexts and found to be acceptable. The results of the most relevant studies will be extracted from Bruhn's (1984) review and from Volume II and summarized below.

Perhaps the most pertinent study was reported by Paige (1974), who looked at the thematic reliability of EMs in comparison to recent memories—in this case memories of summer vacation. Her test/re-test interval was two to four weeks. She found that EMs were thematically stable among her undergraduate sample of 109 subjects and much more stable than recent memories. Eighty percent of the EM test/retest pairs were successfully matched. Winthrop (1958) investigated the long-term temporal stability of EMs for a nonclinical sample of sixty-nine adults over an eight-week period. Using a method of pairing the two sets of EMs, Winthrop reported that sixty-eight percent were correctly matched. Only three of Winthrop's sixty-nine cases reported EMs that were described as "entirely different" (p. 320).

The preceding studies considered temporal stability independent of experimental attempts to effect changes in EM content. Hedvig (1963) employed just such a manipulation: she exposed thirty subjects to success, neutral, and failure expenditures in combination with a friendly, neutral, or hostile interviewer. The stability of EMs was compared with the stability of TAT stories collected at the same time. EMs were found not to be significantly influenced by the experimental manipulation, whereas the TAT stories were, which argues for the greater stability of EM material.

The preceding studies suggest the following conclusions: (1) that EMs are likely to be very stable for most individuals over a period of several weeks to several months; (2) that EMs appear to be more stable than memories of more recent vintage; and (3) that EMs may be more stable and less susceptible to experimental influence than data from other projective techniques, such as the TAT.

Since the EMP consists largely of EMs, it is reasonable to argue that data on the reliability of EMs should apply to the EMP. Paige's (1974) results suggest that more recent memories will also be stable, although perhaps somewhat less so than EMs.

POSITIVE AND NEGATIVE EARLY MEMORIES

As has been discussed under proposition 9 (see Chapter 3), positive EMs reflect wishes and negative EMs fears.

Positive EMs reflect the gratification of major needs in the personality organization. As such, they represent wishes or statements as to how the individual wants his life to be. Such memories have an orienting function in that they contain a self-reminder of what the individual needs to be happy. Additionally, positive EMs have an adaptive function: They preserve in perceptographic form how the individual can meet his needs (see Eisenhower's first EM in Chapter 4).

Consider the following positive EM:

Scoring the winning goal on the playground in soccer. (What is clearest in the memory?) Kicking it. (What is the strongest feeling in the memory?) Happy. (You mean happy that you kicked the winning goal?) Everyone else on my team was happy.

In this memory, we find a crystallization of a wish in perceptographic form of an individual who has strong achievement needs. That this individual has a strong need for approval and acceptance is also clear—he could have focused solely on kicking the goal (achievement) but he indicated that he was pleased because he made everyone else happy (acceptance/affiliation). This memory also serves an orienting function in that it reminds him of what needs to occur for him to be happy.

Achievement needs and acceptance needs are major priorities for this individual.

Whether a given EM is positive or negative depends upon the individual's attitude about what happened. Operationally, the quality of affect is determined from the affect rating scale on the Early Memories Procedure (pp. 9–10). Negative EMs are rated 1 to 3 while positive EMs are rated 5 to 7. Neutral EMs are rated 4.

In a set of EMs, positive and negative memories function as affective counterbalances. It is as if the individual is reminding himself, "Here's how to make me happy and content [positive EMs], and here's how to make me feel unhappy, upset or out of control [negative EMs]." A general rule of thumb is that as the affect in the memory becomes more powerful (positive or negative) the needs in the recollection are likely to assume increasing prominence in the individual's personal hierarchy of needs.

Negative EMs depict the operation of fears. Fears are evoked by a situation that the individual dislikes and avoids or dreads. In negative EMs, a situation occurs that the individual does not know how to resolve or control. As a result, he is flooded with unpleasant affect. The first half of Eisenhower's EM (Chapter 4) is a classic example of this type.

In the following negative EM, the individual focuses on a symbolic loss of function: "I lost my skatekey to my roller skates. (What is clearest in the memory?) Looking for it. (What is the strongest feeling in the memory?) Frustration." When recast as a precis, the memory would read, "I can't get myself going." A feeling of frustration meshes with the action line of the memory—wanting to do something but not being able to. Like the soccer memory, this memory focuses on achievement and mastery needs, but here we find an unresolved issue associated with achievement. The individual acts out his concern that something is not right with him, that something (a "key" element) is missing. By implication, he suggests he needs help—he cannot make his life work (find the key) on his own. He fears mastery situations because he lacks confidence that he can attain his goal on his own.

Early memories that are consistently neutral in affect often indicate an affective blocking, a lack of awareness of feelings, or, in the extreme, an apparent inability to feel anything (alexithymia). Conversely, if an individual experiences feelings in other EMs but rates as neutral what seems an affect-laden event, he is usually selectively blocking feelings around a particular issue. The substitution of inappropriate affect often occurs in delinquent or criminal populations, probably due to the individual's historical failure to bond appropriately with a significant other and develop feelings of empathy. An example of affective substitution is a memory from a violent adolescent who recalled feeling intense pleasure when he got into a fight with a boy, knocked him to the ground and began to kick him repeatedly in the head. Inappropriate affects typically reflect major distortions in interpersonal relationships that commonly have their origins in the early developmental history.

CLEAR AND VAGUE EARLY MEMORIES

If an EM is especially clear relative to other EMs (see EMP ratings, pp. 9–10), it is posited that the individual has energized the recollection to a greater degree with his current thoughts. That is, there is something special about the memory that draws the individual's thoughts to the situation, consistent with the principle of attraction (see Chapter 3). The memory becomes increasingly clear as it is infused with mental energy. A second possibility occasionally occurs. Sometimes the individual is preoccupied with a later incident having a similar form. If so, the earlier incident will be energized by association.

Consider the following as a case in point. This EM, the first given in the EMP, was rated as a 7–5: very positive and exceptionally clear.

> I remember one summer evening in our backyard. I was on my dad's lap. He was sitting on a rocker. The stars were heavy in the sky. My dad singing "The Little White Cloud That Cried." It's all I remember.

This individual had had an extremely turbulent relationship with her father. In addition, she was going through a divorce. She very much wanted to develop satisfying male relationships but was despondent about that ever happening. Her EM reflected a gratification of that wish. No memory could express more clearly or elegantly her wish for male attention and affection and her need to be special. Her relationship with her husband caused her to feel totally ignored—the opposite of special. The irony about the EM, she said, was that she and her father had maintained a generally hostile relationship throughout her childhood and adolescence. The EM pictured one of those rare times when they were close. Thus, the memory expressed her wish to have a warm, affectionate man in her life (father, husband) but her frustration and sadness over not having one.

Vague and unclear EMs, it is believed, result when energy is withdrawn from the EM. The energy loss occurs not because the EM is unimportant; on the contrary, EMs are important by definition. Rather, an energy withdrawal commonly occurs when the individual is not fully prepared to address the issue imbedded in the EM. An analytic model would discuss this process in different terms—repression, displacement of affect, denial, and related defenses. Thus, unclear EMs are usually associated with less awareness and insight and more intense conflict about addressing the unfinished business in the EM.

Whether positive or negative, especially clear EMs reflect something noteworthy for the individual: either a strong wish (positive EM) or a strong fear or dread (negative EM). Extremely vivid, negative EMs are usually traumatic by inspection. Such memories are analogous to a deep rut in the shoulder of a road that begins to envelop a tire as the driver futilely guns his engine. Incredible energy is expended in trying to free the car but to no avail. The more energy committed, the worse the result.

In one exceptionally vivid and very negative EM, a woman recalled having a long-standing crush on a boy. Finally, he asked her for a date. The date went beautifully. He kissed her. She felt like her dream had come true. That night the boy called her on the phone. But to her horror, her father, who was drunk, was in an ugly and abusive mood. He cursed and raged at her mother in the next room. She was totally mortified. The boy never called again or talked to her.

In effect, the memory says, "I have not been able to establish an enduring male relationship [note her low self-esteem as a woman]. My father ruined a relationship that held promise, and I have not yet been able to recover from my humiliation and embarrassment." From another perspective, she blames her father for her problem (her insecurity about dating) and thus is unable to confront the situation as it exists today and resolve it. Her anger and embarrassment have ensnared her and made it impossible for her to grow.

Another 1–5 EM (very clear, very negative) was reported, this time by a handsome, well-educated man who began therapy because he wanted to date but was overwhelmed with anxiety in many social situations. This memory was set at a school function. He briefly left his family to wander around and explore the school with a friend. As he was returning to the function, he left one part of the building to go to another part which was separated from the first by a hallway. When he tried to enter, the door was locked. When he tried to return via the way he came, he was shocked to find the door had automatically locked behind him. He was trapped in the hallway with both exits locked. He panicked with fear that he and his friend would soon exhaust the oxygen supply before anyone came. Terrified, the boys beat on the doors. After a frantic time, someone finally heard the ruckus and came to open the door.

The memory acts out the client's symbolic wish to separate himself from his family and venture out on his own but his panic at having to function independently. His lack of self-confidence when he is removed from the security of his family is reflected. It was his general lack of self-confidence about managing on his own, not a specific insecurity in male/

female relationships, that had to be addressed in therapy, a point made dramatically by his memory.

SIGNIFICANT MEMORIES AND THE EARLY MEMORIES PROCEDURE

How can we tell whether a memory in the EMP is significant?

All memories that appear on the EMP are important. Some memories, however, are first among equals. How can we identify them? The EMP has been constructed with several checks and cross-checks to assess significance. These include the following:

1. The clearest or most important memory/lifetime (memory six in Part I) and the most traumatic memory are believed to be important due to the probe used.

2. Any memory in Part I that is rated as a 1 (very negative) or a 7 (very positive) on the affect scales, given a rating of 5 on clarity, is likely to be highly significant. Affectively charged memories that are clear are believed to be important because they have drawn psychic energy associated with major issues currently in process.

3. Any memory in Part II that emerges several times to different probes (e.g., the first punishment memory is identical to the most traumatic memory and the first EM in Part I) is believed to be significant because it is prominently and redundantly stored in several "locations" in autobiographical memory.

4. Memories that the individual rates as significant (see EMP, p. 11) are likely to be important.

Several protocols will need to be analyzed before a therapist will feel confident deciding which memories are particularly important. The preceding checks will aid in facilitating this process.

INSIGHT AND THE EARLY MEMORIES PROCEDURE

One goal of the Cognitive-Perceptual model is to explicate personality in terms of the contents and organization of autobiographical memory. Until recently, EMs were the primary data base for the CP model. The switch in emphasis from EMs to the EMP is partly predicated upon the belief that clients need to be more actively involved in their therapy. Many individuals can be helped to understand the nature and significance of their problems if they are led through a structured process and asked the right questions (an illustration appears later in Table 5.3). Similar assumptions are embedded in Rogerian therapy, the major

Table 5.3
Summary of an EMP from a Married, White Female in her Forties

Summary	Comments

Part I
EM 1

When I was approximately 5 years old, I remember my mother and father having arguments and my father left. I remember he sat me on his lap and talked to me about leaving, but I cannot remember what he said to me.

Clearest: Sitting on father's lap and his talking to me.
Feeling: Frightened . . . did not want him to leave.
Change: Would like to remember what he said to me.
Age: 5

Precis: Arguments lead to abandonment.
Perception of Self: Vulnerable, not able to function on own.
Perception of Males: Undependable.
Major Issue (unfinished business): Abandonment concerns. Feels vulnerable—does not feel *emotionally self-sufficient. Currently* preoccupied with the threat of loss, just as then.

EM 2

I was living in a different house and a man was visiting my mother (eventually became my stepfather). I did not like him while he was visiting and sat on the floor with a hammer and banged on the floor.

Clearest: Sitting on the floor with the hammer and looking at him.
Feeling: Thought he did not belong there, thought father was better, and mother got rid of him for this man.
Change: Can't think of any change.
Age: 5

Precis: When I don't like someone, I express my feelings through my actions.
Major Issues: 1) That she could not relate to or connect with her mother's friend suggests possible problems with triadic relationships; 2) Her passive-aggressive (indirect) expression of anger (hammering on the floor) suggests problems with direct expression of anger and with assertiveness and self-disclosure.
Process Interpretation: The loss that she felt in EM 1 is amplified by the unsatisfying relationship she is offered as a substitute in EM 2.

EM 3

My mother was married to my stepfather and he was sitting at the kitchen door with a belt and hit me or my sister if we tried to enter the kitchen to talk to our mother. I resisted and he hit me. I ran outside crying and sat by the fence in a corner of the yard and cried, thinking that I would run away and live with my father.

Clearest: Seeing him in the doorway with a belt.

Precis: Possessive of my mother, my stepfather actively interfered with our relationship. When I tried to resist him, he responded aggressively and crushed my attempts to oppose him.
Perception of Self: Needy and impotent.
Perception of Males: In addition to controlling, insensitive and likely possessive--*unreasonable* and harsh, perhaps even brutal (hit her with a belt).

Table 5.3 (continued)

Summary	Comments

Feeling: Felt separated from both parents and alone.

Change: Would like to remember what mother was doing and why he resorted to this type of behavior.

Age: 5-6

Defenses: Escapist fantasies and withdrawal.

Major Issues: 1) Cannot *trust males* to treat her fairly and be sensitive to her needs; 2) Abandonment concerns associated with lack of access to mother.

Process Interpretation: There are problems with her male relationships—her first 3 EMs all concern negative feelings associated with males. The loss that she experienced in EM 1 is amplified by the harsh, insensitive treatment that she experienced from her stepfather.

EM 4

My mother was in the hospital having my new baby brother. I did not know she was having a baby. I thought she was sick and was afraid she might die. I was staying at my grandmother's house and my aunt told me I had a baby brother. I was very happy about that, but she told me that he was so small that they had to put him in a shoebox and he was hanging out the window. I was very upset about that. I never did get to go to the hospital and see my mother or brother.

Clearest: Seeing mother being rushed to the hospital and thinking she might die.

Feeling: Fear.

Change: Remember what my older brother and sister were doing or if I talked with them.

Age: 7

Precis: When I was separated from my mother, I worried about her and was afraid that she might die. Others were not sensitive to my need to see her ("I never did get to go...").

Perception of Self: Emotionally isolated.

Perception of Others: Insensitive, perhaps even cruel.

Major Issues: 1) Abandonment concerns and fear of loss; 2) Trust—doubts that others can be depended upon for nurturance and appropriate care ("they had put (brother) in a shoebox and he was hanging out the window").

Process Interpretation: Her concerns about loss (EM 1) and dependability (EM 3) have generalized to females. The major problem appears to be her *insecure*, vulnerable feelings and the lack of a dependable significant other to assuage her anxiety.

EM 5

My older brother (5 years older) was sick, and the doctor kept coming to the house and telling my mother that he

Precis: Authority figures (physician) can not be depended upon to provide appropriate care.

Table 5.3 (continued)

Summary	Comments

was sick from eating pecans before they were ripe. We had lots of pecan trees. Eventually they took him to a hospital about 50 miles from our house. Again, I was staying at my grandmother's house, and my aunt (she was 10 years older than me) got a phone call and started crying. She told me that my brother had died. He had a ruptured appendix.

Clearest: Aunt's getting phone call and telling me my brother died.

Feeling: I was close to him and couldn't understand why he died. He was 12 years old.

Change: Father came to the funeral (from out of state), and I don't remember seeing him. I wish I could remember seeing him.

Age: 7-8

Memory 6 (A particularly clear or important memory, lifetime)

We were moving to M. because of my husband's job. On the day we finished packing and the movers picked up everything, we were supposed to drive up that night with our son, our dog and parakeet, and fragile household items. At the last minute my husband told me he would have to stay overnight in R. due to unfinished business on his job. I had to drive up alone (I didn't even know how to find our new house, but had directions). I had to be there at 6 a.m. the next morning to meet the movers. I was shocked and wanted him to go with me, but he convinced me he couldn't. A couple of months later through correspondence and long distance calls that he made from there, I found out that my husband had been calling a female friend. I also found out that he had stopped and visited her on his way to M., the day I was there meeting the movers. This was the reason he did not come up with me the night before.

Major Issues: Almost identical to EM 4.

Process Interpretation: Nothing needs to be added from EM 4 except that her concerns about *dependability* and *trust* (note the doctor's diagnosis) have life and death importance. This in turn suggests a high level of stress since so much depends on every decision.

Precis: My husband cannot be depended on to provide help and support; his loyalty and fidelity are much in doubt.

Perception of Self: Emotionally abandoned.

Perception of Others: Self-centered, uncooperative, deceitful, undependable, disloyal.

Major Issues: Similar to those noted in EM 4.

History and Its Role: This set of spontaneous memories can be viewed in two ways. First, it can be argued that the client's EMs demonstrate how issues associated with past relationships spill over into present relationships (husband). According to this approach, the present is constructed consistent with one's experience of past relationship patterns. In her marriage, her husband's actions merely *confirmed* the *negative expectations* that evolved from childhood experiences. Although this

Table 5.3 (continued)

Summary	Comments
Clearest: Fear, shock, and hurt. *Feeling:* Feeling alone, hurt, and deceived, lost trust in what he says and does. *Change:* That we had made the trip together. *Age:* 30	argument is correct in many instances—perhaps most—it is also possible that the individual's *current situation* may cause her to view the past differently so that her recollection of past events mirrors *present concerns.* In other words, it may be just as true that *present experience causes us to view the past the way we do* as the other way around. If this client had been able to establish a satisfying relationship with her husband, she might not have remembered the same events that she recalled on the *EMP.* Placing excessive emphasis on the importance of early experiences tends to produce several biases in how EMs are viewed: 1) We place too much credence in the historical *accuracy* of EMs than we should and; 2) We incorrectly tend to impute *causality* to EMs, rather than regard them as stories that play out issues which are salient for us now (i.e., *correlational* data).

Summary of Rating Scales

	Pleasantness: 7 Point Scale	*Clarity:* 5 Point Scale
EM 1	1: very negative	3: moderately clear
EM 2	2: moderately negative	3: moderately clear
EM 3	1: very negative	3: moderately clear
EM 4	2: moderately negative	3: moderately clear
EM 5	1: very negative	5: exceptionally clear
Memory 6	1: very negative	5: exceptionally clear

Client's rank ordering of significance of memories

1. Most significant: #5
2. Next significant: #1
3. Next significant: #3

Q: Explain why these memories (especially your *most significant* early memories) are significant for you.

A: I think #5 was the most significant memory to me because I felt that my brother was the only person that I could be close to and depend on and he was gone. #1 was significant because I did not want to be separated from my father. #3 was significant because I was being deprived of my mother.

Q: Why do you think that you recall *these* from all your childhood experiences?

A: I think these were traumatic experiences that occurred during my childhood which affect the way I perceive things in my life today.

Table 5.3 (continued)

Interpretation of Rating Scale Data

Clearest EMs (5s on a 5 point scale) are usually the *most significant* memories. Particularly clear memories draw proportionally more psychic energy because the *issue* illustrated by the memory is currently *focal*. One can think of such EMs as being *spotlighted*.

If the clearest memory is also very positive (7 on a 7 point scale), this suggests that a strong need or wish has been gratified—likely a need that is primary in importance for the individual *now*. Such memories contain a self message or reminder to the individual of the form—'this is what you need the most, and here is how this need can be met.' If the clearest memory is very negative (1), this suggests that a *major issue* is being played out, something that the individual is actively trying to work through *now*.

In this protocol two memories are rated as 5s on clarity—EM 5 and Memory 6 (see "Summary of Rating Scales"). The client rates EM 5 as her most significant memory, thus providing independent evidence of its importance. Both are very negative (1s), suggesting a *major issue* in process. The common denominator between memories 5 and 6 involves loss (EM 5) or the threat of loss (Memory 6). Due to the client's preoccupation with loss, there is doubt as to whether she can make a deep emotional commitment to a relationship and risk the kinds of losses and disappointments that she has suffered in the past. Her major issue, then, appears to be a fear of abandonment, which has probably caused her to be *overly cautious* about investing in close relationships—i.e., she tends to isolate herself emotionally. This usual outcome of this pattern is anxiety about forming close relationships and at least a low grade depression associated with unmet dependency and intimacy needs.

Directed memories are requested to determine whether something important was omitted from the *spontaneous* memories in Part I. There are 15 directed memories in all. The five reported here add to what we have gleaned from the spontaneous memories.

Summary	Comments

Part II
First School Memory

I started school at an earlier age by at least 6 months than most other children in my class. This was the first time I had been away from home other than my grandmother's house, and I didn't like being with strangers. One day during class in first grade I saw my brother outside during his recess and I wanted to go outside to be with him. My teacher said no, and I cried, and she finally let me go outside.

Clearest: Seeing my brother swinging outside.

Precis: I feel anxious and insecure when I am away from home and around strangers.

Perception of Self: Insecure and needful of reassurance; sensitive and shy.

Major Issues: 1) It is difficult to meet new people and form new relationships—energy is invested in family and primary relationships; 2) Mild separation problems.

Table 5.3 (continued)

Summary	Comments

Feeling: Wanting to be close to someone that I loved and trusted.

Change: Don't know.

Age: 5

First Family Memory

My sister and I visited my father for the first time since the divorce. I remember how difficult it was after 7 years to be close and affectionate towards him. I also met my stepmother and half sister for the first time. Even though I was happy about visiting him, I had bad feelings about all the changes that had taken place since I last saw him.

Precis: When a separation occurs, I tend to detach myself emotionally and have difficulty reconnecting.

Perception of Self: Emotionally detached.

Major Issue: Difficulty connecting (reconnecting) and feeling comfortable with the relationship; the consequences of separation on her feelings about the relationship.

Clearest: Seeing him at the bus station and feeling like he was a stranger.

Feeling: Permanent detachment.

Change: Could have adapted or accepted the situation.

Age: 12

Traumatic Memory

I found out that I had an ulcer when I was 21 and as a consequence ended up with having surgery when I was 25. I really thought I was going to die just after the surgery while I was in the recovery room and heard everyone rushing and talking about my blood pressure dropping. I had already worried about dying from the surgery the night before I had it and what would happen to my son. Since the surgery I have had continuous gastrointestinal problems due to the surgery. I thought the surgery was to get rid of the problems.

Precis: I followed the advice of my physician, nearly died during the operation, and suffered continually from surgically caused problems ever since.

Perception of Self: Too trusting.

Perception of Others: (authority figures) Untrustworthy.

Major Issue: Cannot trust the advice of an authority figure.

Clearest: Feeling that I was dying.

Feeling: Feeling I trusted that the doctor knew best, but now I think he was wrong.

Change: None.

Age: 25

Table 5.3 (continued)

Summary	Comments

Inappropriate Sexual Memory

As a child my stepfather molesting me and my sister. When he would pick us up he would put his hands inside our panties and tell us not to tell our mother. We did not tell her because we were afraid to and knew she would be hurt and upset. Once when she was in the hospital, and I was 12 or 13, he came into the bedroom where my sister and I shared a bed and started fondling us while we were asleep. I awoke, but pretended to stay asleep because I was afraid of him.

Clearest: Afraid he was going to rape us and didn't know what to do about it.
Feeling: Fear.
Change: Not have it happen.
Age: 12 or 13

Precis: My stepfather molested me and my sister for years, and I was too frightened to say anything.
Perception of Self: Vulnerable, not in control, powerless.
Perception of Others: (male authority figures) Exploitative, abusive, untrustworthy.
Major Issues: 1) Is not able to assert herself, particularly with a male authority figure; 2) Is not able to self-disclose; 3) When victimized and exploited, she is afraid to act.

(Note: This material had not been discussed in therapy before. Furthermore, she had never discussed it with anyone before—not even her sister.)

Fantasy Memory

I wish that I had married someone who was willing to occasionally put me first. I wish I had someone to provide platonic friendship or share platonic friendship. I need someone that I can just be myself with without worrying about being criticized or feeling threatened in the relationship. Sometimes I fantasize that maybe my husband will die and I will still be able to meet someone that could provide companionship, love, support, and unconditional friendship so I can feel relaxed around him. Then I feel guilty about even thinking such a thing. I guess I wish I had married someone different or not married at all. Maybe I married too young to know better.

Major Needs: Acceptance, unconditional love.
Major Issues: 1) Wants to feel free to be herself without fear of being criticized or rejected; 2) Wants an emotionally intimate relationship; 3) Wants to feel valued and important.

(Note: The fantasy memory provides data for the clinician to test his previous hypothesizing, particularly about the major issue and strongest unmet need.)

Client's Interpretation of a Memory
(6th Memory)

I think I recall this memory because all of the years prior to that during our marriage I had excused things that my husband did because he was in school. I was looking forward to the time when he finished school, started working and we could have more children. It became evident to me at that time that things were not going to change and that this was the real personality, not (something) due to the circumstances of being stressed and preoccupied in school. It was also

Table 5.3 (continued)

apparent to me that he had had a relationship or affair with a woman in graduate school. I suspected he was but thought when we moved to another city it ended. She was married and had two children. I suspect that the second child was my husband's.

I think this particular incident has caused me to not have the trust and comfort in our relationship that I need with a mate. This causes me to feel uncomfortable or lonely and unfulfilled in my marriage.

I think a lot of things have happened in our marriage that have caused me to feel lack of support and not have the trust that I would like to have.

(Note: The client's interpretation of this memory, like the fantasy memory, provides an opportunity to validate our hypothesizing, as well as assess the client's degree of insight. The client's choice of memory indicates that she is preoccupied with her marital relationship and is dissatisfied with it in several major respects. Work will be needed in this area because she appears to lack the skills--e.g., assertiveness, self disclosure--to resolve these problems on her own.)

Questionnaire

1. Demographics: Married female in her 40's.
2. (Being seen in treatment?): Yes
   (Connection between reason for treatment and early memories?): Connection is anxiety and stress that I experience and I think it is related to early childhood memories.
3. (What did you learn about yourself?): I am surprised and disappointed that there are so many negative memories. I had never tried to think of them all at one time before or put them in writing.
4. (How much did you learn about yourself?): A moderate amount (rated 4 on a 5 point scale).
5. (Have you ever taken psychological tests before?): Yes
6. (How much time to complete the procedure?): 3 hours or more
7. (How do you view your early memories?): Experiences that reflect my concerns, interests, attitudes and needs now.
8. (How long do you think these particular memories have been your earliest memories?): Most would have been the same since at least adolescence.

Summary of Issues

1. Feels isolated and alone. Concerned about loss and abandonment (EM 1 and first family memory, father's leaving; EM 5, brother's dying).
2. Experiences difficulty making attachments with strangers (first school memory). Takes much time to feel comfortable and connected (first family memory). Primary and family relationships become especially significant since it is difficult to establish new relationships and new attachments (first school memory; fantasy memory). One reason for this difficulty is that she is afraid of *criticism* and *rejection*, which makes her avoid such attachments initially.

Table 5.3 (continued)

3. Has difficulty trusting anyone, even authority figures (memory of inappropriate sexual experience; traumatic memory) who are supposed to be *competent* (EM 5; traumatic memory) and make *her needs* primary (fantasy memory; inappropriate sexual memory; EM 3).

4. Experiences continuing physical ailments as a result of anxiety and problems with stress management (traumatic memory).

5. Has difficulty asserting self—likely with male authority figures in particular (inappropriate sexual memory).

6. Is not able to self disclose material that may be upsetting to significant others (inappropriate sexual memory).

Synthesis of Issues

The core issue (unfinished business) is mostly interpersonal—learning to connect, trust, and depend upon. Although she wants to, she is not comfortable establishing emotionally intimate relationships. One reason is that she is afraid of being criticized and rejected. Another is that she is afraid of abandonment once she establishes a satisfying relationship. A likely consequence of her fear of rejection is her difficulty expressing anger appropriately. Major defenses used when she is confronted with these problems include escapist fantasizing and withdrawal. Peripheral issues involve *self disclosure and assertiveness*, which are likely problematic because of antecedent matters associated with establishing close relationships in the first place. Self disclosure and assertiveness become obstacles to the *intimacy* and *security* that she seeks once a relationship holds the promise of becoming close. An important management consideration involves high levels of *stress* and anxiety, mostly associated with interpersonal issues. Both are serious enough that *somatic* difficulties have resulted. A medical consult needs to be done but with the caveat that any opinion which eventuates is likely to be regarded skeptically by the client.

Awareness

This client is very aware of how she feels and is mostly aware of the nature of her problems and their historical roots. It is therefore appropriate to explore with her what is keeping her from establishing the close relationship that she wants—is it old feelings associated with abandonment and being treated poorly, or are there skills which are lacking? *Self disclosure* and *assertiveness* are almost certainly involved. But her ability to make use of her past experience to pinpoint areas of difficulty for her now puts her in a strong position to address and resolve her problems.

---

difference being that the EMP provides a structure for the individual to reflect on his own as he works with his memories. The process of completing the EMP is believed to have not only diagnostic value but therapeutic value as well since both client and therapist can be clearer about the presenting problem, and what must be done to resolve it.

INTERPRETING AN EARLY MEMORIES PROCEDURE WITH THE COGNITIVE-PERCEPTUAL METHOD

Having applied the Cognitive-Perceptual method to the interpretation of EMs in Chapter 4, we will now analyze a slightly abridged EMP from a woman who was in family therapy about a year before her protocol was obtained. This particular example was chosen because of its teaching value—it is relatively brief, yet it contains a few surprises typical of many EMP protocols.

To conserve space, the protocol will be presented as a table (Table 5.3). In so doing, some material has been slightly abridged. A summary of issues is provided at the end of Table 5.3. The record also includes the first process interpretation of an EMP, which can be compared with the process interpretation for a set of EMs obtained orally at the end of Chapter 4.

CONCLUDING REMARKS

Chapters 4 and 5 have discussed the interpretation of autobiographical memories via the Cognitive-Perceptual method. The memories of several public figures were used to illustrate this process as well as recollections from a clinical population. Those readers who are solely interested in a clinical approach to autobiographical memory should proceed to Volume II, Chapter 10, which explores assessment issues. Those who are interested in doing research with EMs will want to consider Volume II, Chapters 7, 8, and 9, which cover methodological and procedural issues and review prior research.

NOTE

1. The material that follows has been abstracted from Bruhn (1989b) and is used by permission of Psychline Press.

GLOSSARY OF TERMS

Afterthought: An afterthought in an EM is an individual's conclusions regarding the personal meaning of the memory. It typically appears at the end of the plot line of the memory. The events in the memory by this time have been fully described. The afterthought typically consists of some combination of the following: a concluding remark regarding what the experience meant to the individual, how it affected him or her, and how the individual made use of the experience subsequently. The inclusion of an afterthought suggests an ability to reflect about past experience, to extract lessons from that experience, and to make conscious use of these lessons in the present.

Autobiographical Memory: That part of long-term memory that reflects the functioning of the personality. That is, it reflects the individual's sense of self, how the self perceives others, and how the self views the world. It also mirrors what we have come to believe is interesting and noteworthy about the world. The individual's belief system determines the spontaneously accessible content of autobiographical memory, especially how events are constructed and whether particular memories are even available to consciousness. For the most part, autobiographical memory is less concerned with facts and events than it is the individual's opinions and beliefs about these facts and events.

Axioms: Firmly established beliefs that have assumed a status in our worldview analogous to the laws of physics. That is, under ordinary circumstances, axiomatic beliefs function as assumptions, as "givens" not subject to a critical analytical process.

Early Memory: The *preliminary* definition is a recollection of a specific one-time childhood event of the form, "I remember one time . . . " The EM ordinarily describes an event that occurred before the eighth birthday. This definition usually works best with individuals aged 12 to approximately 60. Older or younger individuals may require a different age cutoff. Other considerations, attended to in Chapter 1, may also require modifications or explanation to this definition.

Expectations: Hypotheses or probability statements born of personal experience.

Family Myth: A family myth is a variant of an early memory. It is not an early memory, strictly speaking, because the individual recalls the event as a story told to him by a family member, not a specific event that happened to him personally one time. Typically, the myth itself is highly overworked, with the result that details are either lost entirely or highly stylized as if they were selected or "created" with the message of the memory in mind. These memories are told and retold in the family over a period of years, with the intent, overt or covert, to preserve certain lessons, particularly for the younger generation. These memories are analogous in purpose to tribal folklore that aims to preserve certain vital information for the tribal group so as to guide and direct it and keep it centered on its historical course. Golda Meir's memories provide several examples.

Historical Record: The historical record is not composed of memories per se, but of summaries of those aspects of one's life believed to have interest to others in one's culture. For instance, most Americans, when asked about themselves, will talk briefly about when they were born and where, their parents and how many siblings they had, where they grew up, what schools they attended and graduated from and so on. In many respects, one can conceptualize the historical record as something like a newspaper obituary—facts which we think that others might want to know about us.

Major Unresolved Issue: All of us are working on unresolved issues that are focal for us. The issue may have a normal developmental basis—for example, mastery and achievement concerns are typically ascendant for latency-aged children. Or it may be that an individual is wrestling with a long-term problem that has become entrenched. A major unresolved issue can be identified from a set of spontaneous EMs. When such an issue is resolved, an individual's EMs will change to reflect the unresolved issue that is now focal.

Maladaptive Attitudes: Beliefs that impede or block the satisfaction of needs or the attainment of goals that the individual consciously wants to reach. An example would be a belief that the self is unlovable, which prohibits the individual from establishing a relationship in which he could be loved. An individual must believe that he is lovable in order to be loved, else he will mistrust anyone who professes to love him. (See *Neurotic Behavior*.)

Metaphor: As used with EMs, an "as if" way of communicating present thoughts, feelings, and concerns through the creative reconstruction of early events. For instance, EMs involving an injury to the face usually involve the "as if" communication, "I feel that I have lost face"—that is, that I have been metaphorically injured and been diminished as a result.

Neurotic Behavior: Actions that are self-defeating in the sense that the individual acts so as to make impossible the satisfaction of needs or the attainment of goals that he consciously wants to reach. The underlying basis for neurotic behavior is a pattern of maladaptive attitudes. An example of neurotic behavior would be for a man not to call a woman in whom he is interested, and who has expressed interest in him, because he believes that he will be rejected in the end. (See *Maladaptive Attitudes*.)

Pattern Memory: A recollection of a repeated event, as opposed to a memory of a one-time event of the form, "I remember one time . . ." An example would be: "In the summer after church on Sunday, we used to go to Grandma's for a picnic lunch."

Perceptograph: As applied to early memories, a communication device that conveys concepts *through visually encoded schemas.* Early memories play out concepts symbolically by drawing on purported historical events from our life experience. These memories, whether historically accurate or unconsciously fabricated, depict issues that have a special contemporary relevance—issues in process. Perceptographs preserve our most important needs, our most closely held attitudes, and our perceptions of self, others, and the world, in addition to depicting our major issues in process.

Personality Change: A qualitative change in thinking, marked by a change in expectations, attitudes, and, ultimately, behavior. As thinking changes qualitatively, behavior changes consistent with the new thought process. If the change in personality is positive, behavior becomes more adaptive, and needs that were previously frustrated can now be satisfied because the individual understands what caused him to become frustrated and can handle that situation more adaptively.

Precis: A concise statement of essential points or facts. When used in conjunction with early memories, a precis attempts to capture the basic structure of the memory. In summarizing an early memory, a precis seeks to explicate the individual's basic belief structure concerning the major issue addressed in the early memory.

Process (individual): To attempt to assimilate unincorporated experiences. (See also *Processing (interpersonal)* and *Unincorporated Experiences.*)

Process Interpretation: A process interpretation addresses the question, "What are the psychological bridges that carry us from EM 1 to 2 to 3 to N?" If the first EM presents the major unresolved issue, EMs 2, 3, etc., elaborate that issue and provide information as to how the individual attempts to cope (see Chapter 4 for a process interpretation of a set of oral EMs and Chapter 5 for a process interpretation of an *EMP*).

Processing (interpersonal): What happens when two individuals confront a problem and attempt to negotiate a mutually satisfactory (win-win) solution to that problem. A key element in processing is stating the intention and the problem. For instance, "I would like to help you with the dishes [intention], but every time I do, you criticize what I have done and wash them over. I want to do my share around the house, but what I do doesn't seem to be good enough for you [the problem]. Do you have any ideas as to how we can work this out?"

Report: See pattern memory (synonym). This term is frequently seen in the Adlerian literature.

Repressed Memory: A traumatic memory of which the individual retains no conscious memory. According to CP theory, memories that are repressed or unconscious remain so because they are too painful to deal with. By contrast, memories that are available to consciousness can be processed and worked with in therapy. (See *Trauma* and *Traumatic Memory.*)

Trauma: An event that damaged the individual emotionally in some manner.

The individual might or might not be consciously aware of the event and how it affected him. Events are traumatic, not due to the nature of the event itself, but because of the individual's construction of the event.

Traumatic Memory: A memory of a traumatic event. Some traumatic memories may be readily available to consciousness. Consciously available traumatic memories may be partially or totally processed. (See also *Repressed Memory* and *Trauma*.)

Unincorporated Experiences: Misunderstood or traumatic events that have adversely affected the individual's adjustment. An example would be an individual who believed that father divorced mother and left the family because the client was bad as a child, that the divorce was therefore his fault, and that he was unlovable. In other cases, the traumatic experience is sealed over and preserved just as it occurred at the time so that that it is never reexamined and reinterpreted in light of present adult understandings. In such cases, the event is preserved with the understanding that the individual had at the time, rather than his current adult understanding.

GLOSSARY OF NEEDS

Abasement: To feel guilty when one does something wrong; to feel the need for punishment for wrong-doing.

Achievement: To attempt to be successful or to master; to act to accomplish a goal that is positive and pro-social (as opposed to acting-out or behaving antisocially).

Affiliation: To seek out new friends; or seek to be with current friends so as to share, relate, or experience together. In cases of frustrated affiliation needs, being excluded may be depicted but the underlying need is still affiliation.

Aggression: To be angry; or to attack other points of view; or to attack others physically or to blame others or attack them verbally.

Autonomy: To seek to become independent; or to act so as to separate the self from others; or to set down limits and establish boundaries.

Change: To do new and different things; or to travel, as on vacation; or to look forward to meeting new people.

Dominance: To argue for one's point of view; or to seek to be a leader; or to be elected as a leader; or to supervise others.

Exhibition: To seek to be the center of attention; or to perform, as in plays, talent shows, musical groups or the like.

Heterosexuality: To go out with members of the opposite sex; or to have a crush on a member of the opposite sex; or to become sexually excited by a member of the opposite sex; or to try to become attractive to members of the opposite sex.

These are the needs that I have observed most frequently in EMs. I estimate that this list would account for 90% or more of the needs that occur in a random sample of EMs. Adapted from the Edwards Personal Preference Schedule, the revised manual (1959, Allen L. Edwards, page 11).

Nurturance: To help others when they are in trouble or indisposed; or to treat others with kindness and favor; or to sympathize with others who are sick or hurt; or to be generous with others.

Order: To try to make things neat or organized.

Passive: To watch or observe one's surroundings or others; or to defer to others.

Succorance: To have others provide help when in trouble; to have others act kindly, affectionately, or sympathetically.

BIBLIOGRAPHY

References marked with an asterisk are primarily or substantially concerned with EMs or autobiographical memories.

*Adler, A. (1917). *The neurotic constitution* (B. Glueck and J. E. Lind, Trans.) New York: Moffat, Yard. (Original work published 1912)

*Adler, A. (1927). *Understanding human nature.* New York: Greenberg.

*Adler, A. (1929). *The case of Miss R.* (E. Jensen and F. Jensen, Trans.) New York: Greenberg.

*Adler, A. (1931). *What life should mean to you.* New York: Grosset and Dunlap.

*Adler, A. (1937). The significance of early recollections. *International Journal of Individual Psychology, 3,* 283–287.

*Ansbacher, H. L. (1947). Adler's place today in the psychology of memory. *Journal of Personality, 3,* 197–207.

*Ansbacher, H. L. (1953). Purcell's "Memory and psychological security" and Adlerian theory. *The Journal of Abnormal and Social Psychology, 48,* 596–597.

*Ansbacher, H. L. (1973). Adler's interpretation of early recollections: Historical account. *Journal of Individual Psychology, 29,* 135–145.

*Ansbacher, H. L., & Ansbacher, R. (Eds.). (1956). *The individual psychology of Alfred Adler.* New York: Basic Books.

Bartlett, F. C. (1932). *Remembering: A study in experimental and social psychology.* Cambridge, England: Cambridge University Press.

*Bach, G. R. (1952). Some diadic functions of childhood memories. *Journal of Psychology, 33,* 87–98.

*Bruhn, A. R. (1976). *Earliest memories of being punished as predictors of control stance.* Unpublished doctoral dissertation, Duke University, Durham, NC.

*Bruhn, A. R. (1981). Children's earliest memories: Their use in clinical practice. *Journal of Personality Assessment, 45,* 258–262.

*Bruhn, A. R. (1984). The use of early memories as a projective technique. In P. McReynolds & C. J. Chelume (Eds.), *Advances in psychological assessment* (Vol. 6, pp. 109–150). San Francisco: Jossey-Bass, Inc.

*Bruhn, A. R. (1985). Using early memories as a projective technique: The Cognitive-Perceptual method. *Journal of Personality Assessment, 49,* 587–597.

*Bruhn, A. R. (1989a). *The early memories procedure.* Bethesda, MD: Psychline Press.

*Bruhn, A. R. (1989b). *The early memories procedure manual.* Bethesda, MD: Psychline Press.

*Bruhn, A. R. (1990). Cognitive-Perceptual theory and the projective use of autobiographical memory. *Journal of Personality Assessment, 55,* 95–114.

*Bruhn, A. R., & Bellow, S. (1984). Warrior, general, and president: Dwight David Eisenhower and his earliest memories. *Journal of Personality Assessment, 48,* 371–377.

*Bruhn, A. R., & Bellow, S. (1987). The Cognitive-Perceptual approach to the interpretation of early memories: The earliest memories of Golda Meir. In C. D. Spielberger & J. N. Butcher (Eds.), *Advances in personality assessment,* (Vol. 6, pp. 69–87). Hillsdale, NJ: Lawrence Erlbaum Associates, Inc.

*Bruhn, A. R., & Davidow, S. (1983). Earliest memories and the dynamics of delinquency. *Journal of Personality Assessment, 47,* 476–482.

*Bruhn, A. R., & Last, J. (1982). Early memories: Four theoretical perspectives. *Journal of Personality Assessment, 46,* 119–127.

*Bruhn, A. R., & Schiffman, H. (1982a). Invalid assumptions and methodological difficulties in early memory research. *Journal of Personality Assessment, 46,* 265–267.

*Bruhn, A. R., & Schiffman, H. (1982b). Prediction of locus of control stance from the earliest childhood memory. *Journal of Personality Assessment, 46,* 380–390.

*Burnell, G. M., & Solomon, G. F. (1964). Early memories and ego function. *Archives of General Psychiatry, 11,* 556–567.

*Chess, S. (1951). Utilization of childhood memories in psychoanalytic theory. *Journal of Child Psychiatry, 2,* 187–193.

Corsini, R. J. (Ed.). (1984). *Encyclopedia of psychology* (Vol. 3). New York: John Wiley & Sons.

*Davidow, S., & Bruhn, A. R. (1990). Earliest memories and the dynamics of delinquency: A replication study. *Journal of Personality Assessment, 54,* 601–616.

Derogy, J., & Carmel, H. (1979). *The untold history of Israel.* New York: Grove.

Deutsch, H. (1973). *Confrontations with myself: An epilogue.* New York: W. W. Norton & Co.

*Devereux, G. (1966). Transference, screen memory and the temporal ego. *Journal of Nervous and Mental Disease, 143,* 318–323.

Dreikurs, R. (1950). *Fundamentals of Adlerian psychology.* New York: Greenberg. (Original work published 1923)

Dupuy, R. E., & Dupuy, T. N. (1970). *The encyclopedia of military history: From 3500 BC to the present.* New York: Harper & Row.

*Eckstein, D. G. (1976). Early recollection changes after counseling: A case study. *Journal of Individual Psychology, 32*, 212–223.

Edwards, A. L. (1942). The retention of affective experiences: A criticism and restatement of the problem. *Psychological Review, 49*, 43–53.

Eisenhower, D. D. (1967). *At ease: Stories I tell to friends.* New York: Doubleday.

Fischer, L. (1962). *The essential Gandhi.* New York: Vintage Books.

*Freud, A. (1951). Observations on child development. *Psychoanalytic Study of the Child, 6*, 18–30.

.Freud, S. (1938). Three contributions to the theory of sex. In A. A. Brill (Ed. and Trans.), *The basic writings of Sigmund Freud.* New York: Random House. (Original work published 1905)

*Freud, S. (1950). Screen memories. In J. Strachey (Ed. and Trans), *The standard edition of the complete works of Sigmund Freud* (Vol. 3, pp. 303–322). London: Hogarth Press. (Original work published 1899)

*Freud, S. (1955). A childhood recollection from "Dichtung and Wahrheit." In J. Strachey (Ed. and Trans.), *The standard edition of the complete works of Sigmund Freud* (Vol. 17). London: Hogarth Press. (Original work published 1917)

*Freud, S. (1956). Childhood memories and concealing memories. In A. A. Brill (Trans.), *Psychopathology of everyday life.* New York: The New American Library. (Original work published 1901)

*Freud, S. (1957). Leonardo da Vinci and a memory of his childhood. In J. Strachey (Ed. and Trans.), *The standard edition of the complete works of Sigmund Freud* (Vol. 11). London: Hogarth Press. (Original work published 1910)

*Freud, S. (1960). Childhood memories and screen memories. In J. Strachey (Ed. and Trans.), *The standard edition of the complete works of Sigmund Freud* (Vol. 6). London: Hogarth Press. (Original work published 1901)

*Freud, S. (1971). *A general introduction to psychoanalysis* (J. Riviere, Trans.). New York: Pocket Books. (Original work published 1916)

*Friedman, A. (1933). First recollections of school. *International Journal of Individual Psychology, 1*, 111–116.

Goethals, G. R., & Reckman, R. F. (1973). The perception of consistency in attitudes. *Journal of Experimental Social Psychology, 9*, 491–501.

Gordon, D., & Meyers-Anderson, M. (1981). *Phoenix: Therapeutic patterns of Milton H. Erickson.* Lake Oswego, OR: Metamorphous Press.

*Gordon, K. (1937). Memory viewed as imagination. *Journal of Genetic Psychology, 17*, 113–124.

*Greenacre, P. (1952). A contribution to the study of screen memories. In *Trauma, growth and personality.* New York: W. W. Norton.

Halberstam, D. (1988, March 6). The quiet ambition of Bill Bradley. *Parade*, pp. 4–6.

*Hartmann, H. (1958). *Ego psychology and the problem of adaptation.* New York: International Universities Press.

*Hartmann, H. (1964). *Essays on ego psychology.* New York: International Universities Press.

*Hedvig, E. B. (1963). Stability of early recollections and Thematic Apperception stories. *Journal of Individual Psychology, 19*, 49–54.

The Insight Team of the London Sunday Times. (1974). *The Yom Kippur war.* Garden City, NY: Doubleday.

Iacocca, L. (1984). *Iacocca.* New York: Bantam Books, Inc.

James, W. (1890). *The principles of psychology* (Vol. 1). New York: Holt.

Kelly, G. A. (1955). The psychology of personal constructs (2 volumes). New York: Dutton.

*Kennedy, H. (1950). Cover memories in formation. *Psychoanalytic Study of the Child, 5,* 278–284.

*Kennedy, H. (1971). Problems in reconstruction in child analysis. *Psychoanalytic Study of the Child, 26,* 385–402.

*Kramer, M., Ornstein, P. H., Whitman, R. M., & Baldridge, B. J. (1967). The contribution of early memories and dreams to the diagnostic process. *Comprehensive Psychiatry, 8,* 344–374.

*Kris, E. (1956a). The personal myth. *Journal of the American Psychoanalytic Association, 4,* 653–681.

*Kris, E. (1956b). The recovery of childhood memories in psychoanalysis. *Psychoanalytic Study of the Child, 11,* 54–88.

*Langs, R. J. (1965a). Earliest memories and personality: A predictive study. *Archives of General Psychiatry, 12,* 379–390.

*Langs, R. J. (1965b). First memories and characterologic diagnosis. *Journal of Nervous and Mental Disease, 141,* 318–320.

*Langs, R. J. (1967). Stability of earliest memories under LSD–25 and placebo. *Journal of Nervous and Mental Disease, 144,* 171–184.

*Langs, R. J., & Reiser, M. F. (1961). *A manual for the scoring of the manifest content of the first memory and dreams.* Unpublished manuscript.

*Langs, R. J., Rothenberg, M. B., Fishman, J. R., & Reiser, M. F. (1960). A method for clinical and theoretical study of the earliest memory. *Archives of General Psychiatry, 3,* 523–534.

*Last, J., & Bruhn, A. R. (1983). The psychodiagnostic value of children's early memories. *Journal of Personality Assessment, 47,* 597–603.

*Last, J., & Bruhn, A. R. (1985). Distinguishing child diagnostic types with early memories. *Journal of Personality Assessment, 49,* 187–192.

*Levy, J. (1965). Early memories: Theoretical aspects and application. *Journal of Projective Techniques and Personality Assessment, 29,* 281–291.

*Levy, J., & Grigg, K. (1962). Early memories: Thematic-configurational analysis. *Archives of General Psychiatry, 7,* 57–69.

Liddell Hart, B. H. (1967). *Strategy.* (2nd rev. ed.) New York: Praeger.

*Malamud, D. I. (1956). *Differences in the early childhood memories of authoritarian and nonauthoritarian personalities.* Unpublished doctoral dissertation, New York University.

*Mayman, M. (1984a). Early memories and character structure. In F. Schectman & W. H. Smith (Eds.), *Diagnostic understanding and treatment planning: The elusive connection* (pp. 122–140). New York: John Wiley & Sons. (Reprinted from *Journal of Projective Techniques and Personality Assessment,* 1968, *32,* 303–316)

*Mayman, M. (1984b). Psychoanalytic study of the self-organization with psychological tests. In F. Schectman & W. H. Smith (Eds.), *Diagnostic understanding and treatment planning: The elusive connection* (pp. 141–156). New

York: John Wiley & Sons. (Reprinted from *Proceedings of the Academic Assembly on Clinical Psychology*. Montreal: McGill University Press, 1963, pp. 97–117)

*Mayman, M., & Faris, M. (1960). Early memories as expressions of relationship paradigms. *American Journal of Orthopsychiatry, 30*, 507–520.

Meir, G. (1975). *My life*. New York: G. P. Putnam's Sons.

Moritz, C., et al. (Ed.). (1970). *Current biography yearbook* (31st annual cumulation). New York: H. W. Wilson.

*Mosak, H. H. (1958). Early recollections as a projective technique. *Journal of Projective Techniques, 22*, 302–311.

*Mosak, H. H. (1969). Early recollections: Evaluation of some recent research. *Journal of Individual Psychology, 25*, 56–63.

*Munroe, R. L. *Schools of psychoanalytic thought*. New York: Dryden Press.

Neff, D. (1981). *Warriors at Suez: Eisenhower takes America into the Middle East*. New York: The Linden Press/Simon & Schuster.

*Neisser, U. (1982). *Memory observed: Remembering in natural contexts*. San Francisco: Freeman.

Norman, D. A. (1968). Toward a theory of memory and attention. *Psychological Review, 75*, 522–536.

*Paige, B. K. (1974). *Studies of the content stability of early memories*. Unpublished manuscript, Department of Psychology, Duke University.

Pear, T. H. (1922). *Remembering and forgetting*. New York: Dutton.

Pepper, S. (1970). *World hypotheses*. Berkeley: University of California Press.

*Potwin, E. B. (1901). Study of early memories. *Psychological Review, 8*, 596–601.

Rapaport, D. (1971). *Emotions and memory*. New York: International Universities Press (Original work published 1942)

*Rom, P. (1965). Goethe's earliest recollection. *Journal of Individual Psychology, 21*, 189–193.

*Saul, L. J., Snyder, T. R., & Sheppard, E. (1956). On earliest memories. *Psychoanalytic Quarterly, 25*, 228–237.

*Schachtel, E. G. (1947). On memory and childhood amnesia. *Psychiatry: The Journal of the Biology and Pathology of Interpersonal Relations, 10*, 1–26.

Schrecker, P. (1973). Individual psychological significance of first recollections. *Journal of Individual Psychology, 29*, 146–156. (Original work published 1913)

Stekell, W. (1950). *The autobiography of Wilhelm Stekel*. New York: Liveright Publishing Co.

Stern, W. (1938). *General psychology from the personalistic standpoint*. (H. D. Spoerl, Trans.) New York: Macmillan.

Steven, S. (1980). *The spymasters of Israel*. New York: Macmillan.

*Waldfogel, S. (1948). The frequency and affective character of childhood memories. *Psychological Monographs, 62*, (4, Whole No. 291).

*Winthrop, H. (1958). Written descriptions of earliest memories: Repeat reliability of other findings. *Psychological Reports, 4*, 320.

*Wolfman, C., & Friedman, J. (1964). A symptom and its symbolic representation in earliest memories. *Journal of Clinical Psychology, 20*, 442–444.

NAME INDEX

Adler, A., *xiii*, *xv*, *xvi*, 3, 9, 23, 24–30, 34
Ansbacher, H., 3, 9, 25–27
Ansbacher, R., 3, 26–27

Bach, G., 44–45, 86, 123
Baldridge, B., 31
Bartlett, F., 13, 41, 49, 52–53, 66, 86
Beck, S., 119
Bellow, S., *xviii*, 42, 49, 65, 71, 90, 107
Ben-Gurion, D., 95
Bergson, H., 1
Bradley, B., 62, 98–99
Brill, A., 40
Bruhn, A., *xvii–xviii*, *xix*, 40, 42–43, 49, 65–66, 71, 74, 83, 87–88, 90, 92, 95, 107, 126–27
Burnell, G., 31

Carmel, H., 94
Chess, S., 31
Corsini, R., 123

Darwin, C., 13
Davidow, S., *xviii*, 43, 87–88, 92, 95
da Vinci, L., 29
Derogy, J., 94

Deutsch, H., 114–15
Devereux, G., 28
Dreikurs, R., 52
Dupuy, R., 78
Dupuy, T., 78

Eckstein, D., 40, 123
Edwards, A., 53
Eisenhower, D., *xviii*, *xxi*, 62, 77–85, 88–89, 100, 107, 128–29
Epictetus, 109
Erickson, E., 60
Erickson, M., *xxi*, 6–8, 66, 122
Exner, J., 119

Fischer, L., 97–98
Fishman, J., 31, 40
Ford, H., 96
Freud, A., 24
Freud, S., *xiii*, *xv*, 1, 18, 21, 23–24, 26–30, 34, 40, 47–49, 62, 64–65, 71
Friedman, J., *xvi*

Gandhi, M., 62, 97–98
Goethals, G., 86
Goethe, J., 29
Gordon, D., 6

SUBJECT INDEX

Adlerian theory, *xvii*, 2, 13, 42, 80
  and early memories, 24–30
  differences with Freudian theory
    regarding EMs, 26–28
  similarities with Freudian theory
    regarding EMs, 29–30
Alzheimer's disease, 41
attitudes:
  maladaptive, and autobiographical
    memory, 15–16
  maladaptive, defined, 16
  and perception, 52. *See also* early
    memories, and attitudes
autobiographical memories, as a projective technique, 16–18
autobiographical memory:
  and Early Memories Procedure,
    109–42
  functionally defined, 41
  and how to assess it as a whole, 68
  and how to explore, 2, 47, 109–10;
    use of methods other than the
    Early Memories Procedure, 119–
    21; use of written procedures,
    109–11; use of written procedures,
    major advantages of, 110–11
  and later memories, 97–98
  organizational principles of, 2, 8–9,
10–12, 43–47; activity, 43, 44, 46–
47; attitude, 44, 46; category, 44–
45; mood or state, 43–45, 47; person, 44, 46; place, 44, 46; time, 44,
46
  and principle of adaptation, 3, 42–
    43, 50, 54, 56–59, 63–64, 70
  and principle of attraction, 44, 55–
    56, 69, 99
  and principle of utility, 10, 42–43,
    50, 56, 58, 70
  and relationship between con-
    structed experience and present
    perceptions, 2–3, 55
  three types of, 121–22

behavioral theory, *xvii*
beliefs. *See* attitudes

Cognitive-Perceptual theory, *xvii*, 49–
  50
  and attitudes (or beliefs), 49–50,
    55, 80, 95; axioms, 49; axioms, de-
    fined, 57; primacy of attitudes vs.
    facts, 57
  as contextual model, 50, 60
  early memories, and expectations,

82; and schemas, defined, 53; and schemas, how change occurs, 54 view of human functioning of, 18 what theory explains, 47–48 what powers theory, 43 and wishes, 80 (*see also* early memories, and wishes) contextual theories of personality, 18–20, 48, 60 and philosophical incompatibility with other meta-theories, 60

drives, 47–48
   and defenses, 48
   drive reduction, 47
   sexual, 47–48

early memories (EM):
   and ability to reflect and introspect, 106
   accuracy of, *xv*, 5, 20–21, 24, 42, 66, 122–24
   and affect, 88
   and afterthoughts, 61–107; Eisenhower's and Meir's early memories, 19, 78, 84, 86–88, 97–98; pathological afterthoughts, 86; prevalence of in clinical and non-clinical populations, 86
   and aggression, *xix*, 19–20, 32–33
   and assessing object relations, *xvi*, 33
   and attitudes, *xx*, 25, 28, 61, 71, 98 (*see also* Cognitive-Perceptual theory, and attitudes)
   and axioms, *xx*, 16, 70, 96–97; axioms that appear in pattern myths, 96; maladaptive axioms, 70
   and beliefs (*see* early memories, and attitudes)
   as blueprints, 61
   and CEMSS scoring system, *xix*
   and clarity of recall, 70
   and clinicians' methods of conceptualizing, 42
   and competitive relationships, 105
   and constructing experience, *xx*
   as constructions, 5, 52, 66, 95
   and coping skills, 70, 74, 88, 100–

101; assertiveness, 74; communication, 73; self-disclosure, 74
   and defenses, 72, 74; avoidance, 72, 74–75; denial, 106; withdrawal, 72
   defined, 12
   and delinquency, *xviii*, 95
   and depression, 101; abandonment, 103; feeling different (in a negative way), 105; feeling rejected, 106; feelings of deprivation, 105; lack of confidence (fear of failing), 106; losses, 103–4; overidealization of past, 101, 103
   and determinism (*see* psychoanalysis, and determinism)
   directed, *xix*, 110, 126–27; when stored in multiple content categories, 47
   of Eisenhower, Dwight David, 78–85
   exceptionally early, 5–7
   and fears, 71–72
   first memories: as a template, *xx*, 88; special role of, 9–10, 88, 100
   as focus in therapy, *xx–xxi*
   and frequency of specific recollections by age, 3–4
   and group memories (group identifications), 92–93
   as "headlines," 18
   and hypnosis, *xx-xxi*
   of impotent males, *xvi*
   and interests, 71–72
   and issues in process, 10–12 (*see also* Cognitive-Perceptual theory, early memories, and issues in process)
   and life style, 40, 52–53
   of manic-depressives, 45 (*see also* early memories, and psychiatric diagnosis)
   of Meir, Golda, 85–95
   as metaphors, 76–77
   and narcissism, 101
   and needs, 49, 70–74; achievement or mastery, 72, 74; affiliation, 73–74; aggression, 75

ABOUT THE AUTHOR

ARNOLD R. BRUHN has worked with autobiographical memory since the early 1970s. He formulated the Cognitive-Perceptual theory of personality in conjunction with his work on autobiographical memories, has written many professional papers on the subject, and published *Early Memories Procedure*.

Dr. Bruhn currently maintains a private practice in Bethesda, Maryland, and lectures frequently on the assessment of autobiographical memory, the use of early memories in psychotherapy, and the application of Cognitive-Perceptual theory to psychotherapy.